Chuck Taylor, All Star

CONVERSE
ALL STAR
Chuck Taylor
®

The **True Story**
of the **Man** behind the
Most Famous
Athletic Shoe
in **History**

Abraham Aamidor

Indiana University Press   Bloomington and Indianapolis

This book is a publication of

Indiana University Press
601 North Morton Street
Bloomington, IN 47404-3797 USA
http://iupress.indiana.edu

Telephone orders   800-842-6796
Fax orders   812-855-7931
Orders by e-mail   iuporder@indiana.edu

The paper used in this publication meets the minimum requirements
of American National Standard for Information Sciences–Permanence
of Paper for Printed Library Materials, ANSI Z39.48-1984.

Manufactured in the United States of America

Library of Congress Cataloging-in-Publication Data

Aamidor, Abraham.
  Chuck Taylor, all star : the true story of the man behind the
most famous athletic shoe in history / Abraham Aamidor.
      p. cm.
  Includes bibliographical references and index.
  ISBN 0-253-34698-3 (cloth : alk. paper)
  1. Taylor, Chuck, 1901–1969. 2. Basketball players—
United States—Biography. I. Title.
  GV884.T38A36 2005
  796.323'092—dc22   2005016232

1 2 3 4 5 11 10 09 08 07 06

Contents

Foreword
by Dean Smith

When Abraham Aamidor called from Indiana to interview me for his new biography of Chuck Taylor, I was amazed that someone had not written one years before, because Taylor was such an important figure in America's basketball history. Obviously, I'm extremely pleased that Abe is filling this void. It's a service to all who love basketball and its roots.

One of my earliest memories of Chuck Taylor is about the shoe, not the man. Prior to the start of practice for our 1951–52 University of Kansas basketball team, coached by Dr. Forrest C. (Phog) Allen, team members were given new red "Keds" basketball shoes, which surprised us all. We had always worn the "Chucks," but Dr. Allen insisted that we switch to "Keds." After all, the crimson color in that shoe was, and still is, one of the colors for the University of Kansas athletic teams. I didn't understand why Dr. Allen changed our shoes, because most of us thought the "Chucks" were the best basketball shoe of that day, as well as by far the most popular.

Only recently did Abe explain to me why Dr. Allen outfitted our team for "Keds" and dumped the "Chucks." Taylor and Dr. Allen had put on a basketball clinic together, and Chuck, with his outstanding and unusual passing skills, had apparently upset Dr. Allen with his showmanship. It was supposed to have been a clinic on offense and defense, but Chuck apparently stole the show with his artful passing. Dr. Allen was a great coach, motivator, and speaker, but he didn't like to be upstaged. Our Kansas team went on to win the NCAA championship in 1951–52 but take it from me it wasn't because of the shoes. (Since Indiana University Press is publishing this book, I should point out that in 1953, my senior year, our Kansas team lost to Indiana in the final game 68-67, and we were wearing the same red shoes!)

In 1956–57, I became assistant basketball coach at the new Air Force Academy, then in its second year. The head coach was Bob Spear, one of the greatest teachers ever to coach college basketball. Bob wanted our players to wear Converse Chuck Taylor All Stars. However, it wasn't that simple in the Air Force. We couldn't just order what we wanted and be done with it. We had to give specifications on the product in question, and then the government would decide which supplier best met the specifications. In other words, a clear definition of "Red Tape." Bob Davies, the former great pro player, was the salesman for Converse and told us how to place the order in such a way that only Converse could meet the specifications. We even went so far as to request Chuck Taylor's autograph on the shoes. Unfortunately, they arrived as a basketball shoe named "Lacrosse," so our basketball cadets had to wait until their senior season to wear the "Chucks."

It wasn't until 1959 that I came to know Chuck Taylor well, when I became Frank McGuire's assistant coach at North Carolina. Chuck was a regular visitor to Chapel Hill, and, of course, our team wore his Converse shoes. Chuck traveled often in the South, and when possible, he stayed with his special friends, Jimmy and Tassie Dempsey of Wilson, N.C. He met the Dempseys when Jimmy was a major in the Air Force in World War II and they remained close friends. Even when

Foreword

Chuck married at a late age, his wife Lucy traveled with him and stayed with the Dempseys.

My first year as North Carolina's head coach was the 1961–62 season. Chuck and the Dempseys came by and invited me to dinner. Over the meal, Chuck told me he had a new, weighted shoe that was designed for early-season training to strengthen the legs. He claimed that training in the heavy shoes would make the players quicker and faster once they moved back to the "Chuck All Stars." Chuck made a pretty big deal out of it, telling me that he was going to have only two teams try out these new shoes in the first week of practice. North Carolina was one of the teams, and the other would be out west. I thought this was a high compliment to Carolina's basketball program, and agreed to have our players practice in the weighted shoes.

After three days of wearing them, my starting backcourt players were limping with groin injuries. Senior guard Donnie Walsh, president of the NBA Indiana Pacers, and junior guard Larry Brown, head coach of the New York Knicks, were sidelined for a few practices. Other players on the team complained of minor soreness in the groin, but continued to practice in the weighted shoes. Larry Brown still talks about how we never hesitated to try new things on offense and defense at Carolina, but the weighted shoes might not have been our greatest idea.

I saw only one Chuck Taylor clinic, which was enough to convince me of his great passing skills. He thoroughly enjoyed feeding the post players with his fakes and cunning passes. He handled the ball extremely well. Chuck always started his clinics by showing coaches how to teach their players to feed the post. In many ways, basketball was Chuck's life. He wanted to play the game when he was young, and then talk about it as he became older. Chuck was important to basketball, as he performed thousands of clinics and surely helped coaches learn better ways to teach the game.

I was told that some college athletic directors called Chuck and asked him to recommend coaches for their school. I understand he was instrumental in bringing a fellow Hoosier, Everett Case, to the head coaching position at N.C. State from his job as a high school coach in Indiana. Coach Case brought many talented Indiana high school basketball players with him to N.C. State, and they were champions of the Southern Conference and the Atlantic Coast Conference for a number of consecutive years. Everett's first job was assistant coach at Chuck's old high school in Columbus, Indiana, and they were just a year apart in age. Chuck's relationship to the state of North Carolina dates back to 1925, when he gave his first clinic at N.C. State under Coach Gus Tebell. Chuck spent a lot of his time in North Carolina, so we like to call him an adopted son.

The subtitle of this biography reads: "The true story of the man behind the most famous athletic shoe in history." For decades the Converse Chuck Taylor All Star *was* the most famous athletic shoe. But as most of you know, the shoes named for a fellow by the name of Michael Jordan, who played ball at and graduated from Carolina, may now share that title. I'm sure Chuck wouldn't mind me mentioning this.

It is fitting and correct that Chuck Taylor is in the Naismith Basketball Hall of Fame in Springfield, Massachusetts, as a contributor. He gave his life to basketball, and many in basketball shared their knowledge and love of the game with him. For players on great teams, as well as those who didn't make the cut on their high school teams and played pickup games nights and weekends, Chuck Taylor gave you what for many years was the favorite athletic shoe in the world. He was indeed a man of basketball.

Chapel Hill, North Carolina
September 22, 2005

Foreword

Acknowledgments

Acknowledgments are written for the people who actually help with a book, typically with no ulterior motive or expectation of any reward. Grady Lewis, Joe Dean, and John Wooden were the closest associates of Chuck Taylor I found, and each was most generous with his time. Other sources who personally knew Chuck whom I was able to locate and interview are cited in the text. Alan Kimbrell was almost benevolent in allowing me access to his late mother's home and files. Alan's mother, Lucy Taylor Hennessey, was Chuck's second wife, and Lucy's former private nurse, Gloria Schroeder, was most helpful during my visit to Port Charlotte, Florida, to view the estate. Chris Doyle, a publicist for Converse, Inc., and David Maddocks, vice president of marketing, arranged access for me to company archives in North Andover, Massachusetts. Larry Weindruch, a spokesman for the National Sporting Goods Association, gave me useful contacts and background on traveling salesmen in the old days.

Terri Wall, a librarian at the *Indianapolis Star,* gave me useful tips in searching old newspaper records. Greg Murphy is a professional researcher who did some work for me at the National Archives and Records Administration. Dick

Reynolds, unofficial historian in Richmond, Indiana, was helpful, as were newspaper editor Harry McCawley and librarian Ronda Brown from Columbus, Indiana. Michael Brooslin, curator at the Naismith Memorial Basketball Hall of Fame in Springfield, Massachusetts, and Robin Deutsch, director of library services, were gracious hosts during a day I spent in their archives. Jim Durham of Georgetown College, Mike Odneal of Westminster College, as well as sports information officers at Georgetown University, Western Kentucky University, North Carolina State University, the University of North Carolina, Purdue University, The Ohio State University, and the University of Wisconsin also were helpful in my research. Diana Lenzi provided me with two wonderful, rare photos of Chuck's wartime basketball team. Maria Garcia and Terry Eberle, former editors at the *Indianapolis Star,* were instrumental in allowing me to modify my hours so I could pursue this project while still having at least a part-time income at work. Bob Rich was helpful in the editing. Sportswriters Elliott Almond, Adam Schefter, Steve Salerno, Bob Hammel, and Jay Weiner, and Mark Shaw all had useful suggestions for me as I sought to market this book. Bob Sloan and Janet Rabinowitch of Indiana University Press were professional at all times. And, at the risk of sounding gratuitous, I have to thank my wife, Shirley, and sons, Joseph and David, for putting up with me while I worked on this project.

ABRAHAM AAMIDOR
Carmel, Indiana
July 2004

Acknowledgments

Chuck Taylor, All Star

Introduction

It's a Wednesday night, March 19, 1919, in Columbus, Indiana, a prosperous manufacturing and agricultural center of about 9,000 souls forty-five miles southeast of Indianapolis. The recent hard winter has not quite broken. Inside a two-story, red brick government building, in the high-ceilinged second-floor auditorium, scores of basketball fans have gathered to see a doubleheader: The Indianapolis Em-Roes Juniors are playing the Concordia Club in a warm-up match, and the Columbus Commercials, the local semi-pro team, are about to knock off a nearby military squad, the Camp Grant Five, by a score of 45-30. "Swamped" the soldiers, a newspaper reporter was to write the next day.[1] It was just another basketball exhibition in just another small Indiana town, hardly a major sporting event in 1919, yet the local press was there. Why?

It could be they came to watch local *wunderkind* Charlie Taylor, a seventeen-year-old high school senior and captain of the Columbus High School Bull Dogs, which had just returned from the State High School Athletic Association single-class boys basketball tournament in West Lafayette the previous weekend. Though Taylor and his comrades were eliminated in the quarterfinal round, the city had feted the team Tuesday evening in that very auditorium, followed by a candlelight procession through downtown streets that attracted hundreds. The Camp Grant Five game was Charlie Taylor's inauguration in professional sports. He did not score, and he only played the last three minutes in what was essentially a walkover. It should have been a forgotten, inconsequential exhibition game, a blip in time in the history of sports, except that the (Columbus, Ind.) *Evening Republican* had chosen to cover the event and report on the young basketball pilgrim's progress. Taylor's presence on this court while still in high school signaled his promise and his ambition, and the media's attention foreshadowed a mutual love affair that was to last nearly fifty years, though Taylor's prominence faded into obscurity even before his death in 1969.

Chuck Taylor, as the world would come to know young Charlie, was at the forefront of popularizing the game of basketball to the masses. Beginning in 1932, more than 750 million pairs of gym shoes known as the Converse Chuck Taylor All Star would be sold, making Taylor's signature arguably the single most successful endorsement of sports equipment anywhere in the world, ever. Similar shoes from U.S. Rubber ("Keds"), B. F. Goodrich ("P. F. Flyers"), and others also sold millions, and in the 1950s kids aligned with their favorite brands much as their parents chose Ford over Chevy. Air Jordans may be more famous today, but "Chucks" remain virtually unchanged after decades: rubber-soled, double-wall canvas body, and the circular ankle patch with a bright blue star in the middle and Chuck Taylor's signature across it. The shoe, and the ankle patch, are pop art today. They are cultural icons, whether for grunge youth and alternative lifestyles or for country boys who remember skipping over gravel roads in them in their youth. The shoes especially are associated with the formative years of basketball in this country. They were standard fare for high school, college, and professional basketball players well into the 1960s, when their popularity gave way to leather shoes from Adidas, Puma, Reebok, and, in an ironic twist, Nike. One says "ironic" because Nike, the international shoe behemoth that gained steam with its running shoe in the late 1970s, finally purchased Converse, Inc., in 2003, exactly ninety-five years after Marquis Converse founded the Converse Rubber Shoe Company in Malden, Massachusetts.

Yet Chuck Taylor remains the most famous name in sports that no one knows anything about. Sports journalist Frank DeFord, in both a National Public Radio commentary and a written essay in 2003, remarked how he didn't even know there was a real Chuck Taylor until former basketball player and former Converse employee Rod "Hot Rod" Hundley offered to introduce him to Taylor in the mid-1960s. DeFord thought the name "Chuck Taylor" was a marketing tool, much like "Betty Crocker" is for foods. Other sports journalists also have marveled in print how little is known about Chuck.

Bob Sherrill, a columnist for the *Durham Morning Herald*, found the whole persona mythical. "Taylor is still as insubstantial as the Wandering Jew; he lurks everywhere as a name and a suggestive, putative existence, but who is he?" Sherrill asked in 1981. "Who was he? Where did he come from? Is he flesh and blood?"[2]

Or, as *Orange County Register* journalist John Hughes

once brilliantly declared, "The man's biography begins and ends with his name."[3]

I, too, wondered who Chuck Taylor was. In February 2001 I had been asked to write a story about Converse and about Chuck Taylor. I was a reporter at the *Indianapolis Star* and had been known to wear my white (natural unbleached, to be more precise) high-top Chuck Taylors to work in mild weather, even when it wasn't casual Friday. Chuck Taylor was just some old basketball player, I figured. Except that, somehow, I knew he was from Indiana, and I had seen a couple of the old Converse Basketball Yearbooks in my youth. I always wanted to have my picture in that yearbook, like players from hundreds of high school and college teams did each year. But who was Chuck Taylor, really? Usually there's a story behind any and all sports legends that's pretty well documented, even if parts of the "story" are mythical. For example, early Notre Dame football coaching legend Knute Rockne is remembered in detail. He was real, even if his persona today is larger than life and the text of some of his inspirational pep talks no longer quite accurate. I was to discover that very little had ever been written about Chuck Taylor, though, and much of what existed was wrong. I wanted to know more about this Taylor and I set for myself a quest, not unlike those modern anthropologists and world travelers one sees on public television who personally climb the Alps to unravel the secrets of a 5,000-year-old frozen Neanderthal, or who ride the second-class rails in India because they just have to follow in the footsteps of some ancient renowned religious leader.

My quest lasted three years, on and off, and took me to Ohio, Maryland, Massachusetts, Florida, California, and through my own backyard, which is to say across Indiana. I discovered that part of the Chuck Taylor mythology was just that—myth—but also that the truth, warts and all, was much more interesting. Chuck was a great, great basketball coach—a part of his biography completely forgotten in recent decades—and he was instrumental in getting other basketball men top jobs at important universities. For example, he is legitimately credited with helping fellow Hoosier Everett Case obtain the head basketball coaching job at North Carolina State University after World War II and seeding basketball throughout what was to become the Atlantic Coast Conference. Chuck was involved for years in making large payments to the important National Association of Basketball Coaches, which bought loyalty for Converse products, leading to the company's dominance in the marketplace. Chuck also was instrumental in bringing African American basketball personalities Earl Lloyd and John McClendon to Converse during different stages in their careers, and the Converse Basketball Yearbook featured black athletes and coaches in perfectly respectful articles years before it became commonplace to do so. Chuck knew coaches everywhere, but he was to have a strained relationship at the very end of his life with fellow Hoosier, longtime friend, and legendary UCLA basketball coach John Wooden.

In the 1920s, Chuck was involved with "industrial league" basketball, which was more prominent in America than "professional" basketball at the time. Industrial league athletics in general were seen by corporate America as bringing the benefits of sport and competition to the working man and woman just as they did for the middle classes in YMCAs and colleges across the country, but they also were decidedly designed to keep working people away from Bolshevism and communism.

Chuck Taylor was nationally known during his glory years from the 1930s through the 1950s as a former pro basketball player, as a businessman, as a teacher who put on thousands of "Fundamentals of Basketball" clinics in high school and college gyms across the country, as the creator of a highly regarded annual college basketball All-American list, and as a top-flight golfer.

He also had three championship seasons—not years when he actually won a title, but the championships he chased and almost won, first as a high school boy, then as a basketball player on an important industrial league team, then as a wartime coach.

Chuck's basketball clinics often were covered by the local press in small towns as major news events. Chuck also would personally call on retail sporting goods stores across the country—that personal service, along with his clinics, are what really made his name and made Converse Chuck Taylor All Star shoes so popular.

Small-town and neighborhood sporting goods stores, the kind that personally outfitted local high school and college teams, and which changed their window displays with the sports seasons, are almost all gone now. They died with Chuck Taylor, in a sense.

Yet Chuck Taylor was real—he would come into a store, or walk onto a gym floor in casual togs and his own brand of shoes, with a leather-wrapped basketball tucked under his arm, or he'd give a little newspaper interview and rank the best teams and players in the country because he personally knew who the best players and coaches were—and it was real. Not corporate, not computerized. Real.

"Chuck Taylor" may be pop art or a cultural icon today, but newspaper articles and advertisements in the 1930s touted Chuck's arrival in town for one of his clinics, which often were accompanied by "talking movies" of the previous year's college basketball tournaments and as such were a big attraction. No admission ever was charged and no commitment to buy the shoes was required. He just sowed the seeds of basketball's popularity. Taylor did thousands of these clinics over a span of more than three decades; they typically drew an average of 300 or 400 guests, but sometimes many more. Chuck almost certainly taught more people basketball live and in person than any better-known basketball coach who ever lived.

Chuck also was a key figure in the often overlooked U.S. Army's Special Services Division, which had a leading role in building morale and physical fitness for soldiers during World War II. Chuck was coach of the Wright Field (Ohio) Army Air Force "Air-Tecs," arguably the greatest service basketball team in history. Other wartime basketball or football coaches who also served under the broad umbrella of the Special Services Division or in similar Navy programs included Paul D. "Tony" Hinkle, the longtime Butler University basketball coach, and Paul "Bear" Bryant, who went on to fame as the University of Alabama football coach.

The Air-Tecs toured the country during the 1944–45 season competing against both college teams and other military squads, winning well over 90 percent of their contests. Star players on the team included John Schick, Dike Eddleman, Ed Sadowski, Bruce Hale, John Mahnken, Al Negratti, Chris Hansen, and others, all of whose names will be recognized by serious students of the game and its history. Nearly all were consensus college All-Americans and/or went on to successful NBA playing or coaching careers. Chuck personally recruited several of them to his squad, wangling transfers from other military basketball squads when necessary.

There's another reason to look closely at what Chuck and all the other professional athletes and coaches did during the war, for it will be argued that World War II taught all Americans to play basketball. The Special Services Division mandated a definitive, standardized basketball rules book in

1943 for all to use, and Special Services and a related Navy program promoted basketball everywhere because it was a cheap and effective morale booster and fitness regime. It is believed that this book was the first single, authoritative, national book of basketball rules. Basketball historians are well aware that prior to World War II college and pro teams often had divergent rules, and different pro leagues also had their own rules. Prior to World War II, college basketball far outshone professional basketball in popularity, yet college basketball had an elitist air—after all, "college men" played it—while pro basketball was more like roller derby or pro wrestling is today. The military brought basketball to the masses.

There are problems with the Chuck Taylor "story," however. For starters, the previous research does not correctly identify which pro teams Chuck played for. "We're always hearing that [Taylor] spent 11 or 12 years playing ball professionally, but we've spent 25 years researching pro ball and we've never seen his name in a box score yet," author and basketball historian Bill Himmelman once said.[4] Himmelman compiles old basketball statistics both for the NBA and his own research company and his suspicions are not completely unfounded. Chuck has routinely been called a veteran of the "world champion" Original Celtics and "Olympic champion" Buffalo Germans, two Hall of Fame teams famous in America when Chuck was coming of age and beginning his own basketball quest in the 1920s. Proving a negative is never easy, but Chuck never played for either team, though he certainly had a respectable basketball career in his own right.

Other errors in the previous research include how many times Chuck was married, how he was paid at Converse, why the shoes were named after him, and so on. The Converse All-Stars barnstorming team, which Chuck both coached and starred on, was completely ignored in the previous research.

The existing information was full of red herrings. Most of the previous "sources" simply relied on each other for information, regurgitating the same incorrect details and mostly perpetuating myth.

Some brief bios (always brief) do speak of Chuck's marriage late in life to the love of his life, Lucille Taylor Hennessey. It was a second marriage for both. Lucy traveled with Chuck to many of his basketball clinics in the 1960s and hosted a luncheon for coaches' wives during the Final Four tournament for several years after he died. The real "story" here, though, is that Chuck Taylor came to Fulton, Missouri, one day in 1957 to give a basketball clinic at Westminster College and ran off with the athletic director's wife, Lucy, who taught English at nearby William Woods College. It turned out to be a major scandal in the life of both Westminster and William Woods. People in Fulton still remembered the scandal as of 2003.

Chuck was legendary for roaming the country in big, expensive cars of the day, staying in hotels 365 nights a year and putting everything on an expense account, which Converse would pay. This part of "the story" is mostly true. There is evidence he lived out of two trunks in the Converse regional warehouse in suburban Chicago for many years—one trunk with winter clothes and one with summer clothes. Yet he maintained a home address with his parents in Columbus at least through the 1930s, though he probably did not live there full-time, and he owned a home in Los Angeles throughout much of the 1950s. He shared the Los Angeles home on fashionable Bellagio Road with his first wife, former actress Ruth Alder.

One token of Chuck's life that barely survives, but which was anticipated every fall by generations of boys and girls across the continent, was the beautiful Converse Basketball Yearbook, which ran from 1922 until 1983. In a single volume, fans would see stories and pictures of college and high school basketball teams, and in later years the pros were added. There never was a cost for coaches to place a team photo and short summary of the past season in that book. Imagine, you and Bob Cousy in the same book, you and Chuck Taylor in the same yearbook! The covers in later years had beautiful illustrations in the style of Norman Rockwell's covers for the *Saturday Evening Post,* though done by other artists, and the full-text articles, especially in earlier years, were by important basketball coaches such as Holman or Case or Notre Dame basketball coach George Koegan, who railed in the 1931 edition that "basketball officiating hinders sport." By the 1950s, famous African American coaches such as McClendon (Tennessee State) wrote technical articles on how to play the game. These men taught the game of basketball to high school and small-college coaches and players everywhere.

The story of Chuck Taylor also is the story of Converse, Inc., which went bankrupt in 2001. I wanted to know how the company that made the most successful sports shoe in American history could crash and burn so dramatically, how something so beloved and iconic could end up so forlorn. An Appendix to this book includes a full chapter on the history of the company—the rise and fall and rise of Converse, which was sold to Nike, Inc. in 2003. The Converse factory in Lumberton, North Carolina, was the last factory in America to produce this type of athletic shoe when it was shut down in 2001, throwing 475 persons out of work. Their jobs were shipped first to Indonesia, then to China, and the history of Converse also is a clear marker for the loss of America's manufacturing base in general. Can America really become the middleman of the world, simply marketing other people's efforts? It's beyond the scope of this book to make such predictions, but it sure looks like corporate America and many of the nation's political leaders think this is plausible.

Things always change, and we can argue whether the change is for the better or for the worse. The following chapters tell the story of a man, a company, a sport, and even a nation that either are no more or no longer are what they once were. I believe most people will conclude that basketball is far, far better off today because Chuck Taylor was real, and that the game now suffers because no legendary men like Chuck Taylor remain.

1.   **Hall of Fame**

Five aged men stood on the podium in the hotel ballroom in Springfield, Massachusetts that early spring evening in 1969. Each was dressed in a business suit, tie, and heavily lacquered leather shoes—a far cry from their usual togs on a hardwood court, where each had fought his way to recognition as a great basketball icon. This was the Naismith Memorial Basketball Hall of Fame induction, and about 400 guests, sportswriters, and local dignitaries had come to witness one of the greatest "classes" yet in the history of the Hall of Fame.

Arnold "Red" Auerbach, an early coach of the now for-gotten Washington Capitols but better known for his nine NBA championships with the Boston Celtics in the 1950s and 1960s, was an inductee. Henry G. "Dutch" Dehnert, a star of the legendary, pre–modern era Original Celtics from New York City in the 1920s, also was inducted.

College coaches Henry P. "Hank" Iba, from Oklahoma A&M, and controversial Kentucky coach Adolph F. Rupp also were inducted. Rupp has a basketball arena named for him in Lexington; they honor their basketball icons in Kentucky like they revere saints in some religions.

Standing on the podium to the far right of these well-known basketball men was Chuck Taylor, whom one might call the father of the high-top canvas basketball shoe, though he really wasn't. Whereas Auerbach, Dehnert, Iba, and Rupp were touted for games won or points scored on the basketball court, Chuck's credits were more amorphous. He was inducted as a "Contributor" to the game of basketball.

Yet his contributions were many. By 1969 the Converse Rubber Shoe Co., as it originally was known, had sold nearly 400 million pairs of shoes with the emblematic "Chuck Taylor" signature on the small, rubber ankle patch found on each. The name "Chuck Taylor" on a basketball shoe was like "Duncan" on a yo-yo, or maybe "sterling" on silver. And Chuck had personally hosted or directed approximately 4,000 basketball clinics in high school and college gyms over the previous forty-seven years, bringing the fundamentals of the game, rules, and basic strategies to inexperienced coaches and aspiring players all across the country. For years, his annual college All-American picks were the most watched in the country.

"Red" Auerbach was the only legend from the class of 1969 still alive in 2004. The cantankerous ex-coach, who still held an executive post with the Boston Celtics, maintained an office near his Washington, D.C.–area home, where he'd dress every morning and go to work for two or three hours and chew the fat with a steady stream of sportswriters, authors,

13

Hall of Fame

and ordinary fans who managed to find him. He remembered the induction in Springfield and the surprise nomination of Chuck Taylor, who was not known as a great player, or as a coach at all.

"I'm looking at a picture of [the ceremony] right now," Auerbach said, speaking in a voice that had become raspy and abrasive over the years, perhaps from yelling at players or referees, or even sportswriters. "It was at a club in town. The Hall of Fame wasn't big enough. Iba and Rupp were friends of mine. Chuck I just knew. And Dutch Dehnert was there—he was older than I, of a different era. But Chuck fit in. It was one player, three coaches, and a contributor."

Each inductee stood under a large plaque hanging from a wall that featured a portrait in relief, plus the honoree's name. Chuck stood with almost serene aplomb in the photo—revealing nothing of the glad-handing, gregarious persona one might expect of the man. Chuck, who had started out life in the early pre-dawn of basketball in America with only one ambition in life—to be a great player in this new, exciting, barnstorming sport—had achieved success through the back door, as a "Contributor." His early years had been ones of relentless pursuit of a fast-paced game and a short write-up in a local newspaper. Finally, he was getting his due.

They say basketball was invented in 1891 by James Naismith, a Canadian-born lacrosse player who taught physical education at a YMCA training school in Springfield, the same city that is home to the Basketball Hall of Fame. But the game really grew up in Indiana in the first years of the twentieth century, in a place of tall corn rows and lanky teenagers throwing a ball at a hoop nailed to the side of an old barn. That's where Chuck Taylor grew up.

Chuck Taylor could not have known he'd be a Hall of

Famer one day when he joined the strong Columbus High School Bull Dogs basketball team in 1915, but neither could an amazing cadre of other Indiana youths from the same era, all of whom ended up in the Naismith Memorial Basketball Hall of Fame, and all of whom had one other thing in common—they all personally knew, and in some way were touched by, Chuck Taylor himself. In one of those rare confluences of history, a group of individuals, all with Indiana connections, all with roots in the first years of the twentieth century, and all with close ties to each other long before any were famous, played the game of basketball, shaped it and spread its gospel from coast to coast before their days were done. It was like the French Impressionist school of the late nineteenth century—how could Renoir and Monet and Degas and all the rest not only be great painters, but close contemporaries in time and place as well? So, too, with these native Hoosiers.

Consider these Hall of Famers: Chuck Taylor, the basketball shoe icon from tiny Azalia and Columbus, Indiana; John Wooden, the Purdue University star and legendary UCLA coach who was one of the few men in the history of the game to be inducted both as a player and a coach; Charles "Stretch" Murphy, who also was an All-American selection with Wooden at Purdue University in the early 1930s and was the man who nominated Chuck to the Hall of Fame in 1969; Clifford Wells, who coached a state championship team at Bloomington High School in 1919 while still an undergraduate at Indiana University; Everett Dean, who led IU's basketball team during its first run to glory in the 1920s; Everett Case, an intense coach who was twice banned by the Indiana High School Athletic Association for recruiting violations before landing the head coaching job at North Carolina State after World War II; Tony Hinkle, the Butler University and Great Lakes Naval Training Station legend; Robert "Fuzzy"

Vandivier from the Franklin (Ind.) College "Wonder Five" teams; and Purdue coach and National Basketball League commissioner Ward Lambert, who was born in South Dakota but raised in Indiana. Not one of these men can individually claim credit for wedding America to the game of basketball for good, but collectively they could. And Chuck Taylor was part of that collective, every bit as important as any of the other hoop architects, recalled John Wooden, the only one of this group who survived all the way to the twenty-first century.

"The first time I saw [Chuck], I think it was back in high school," Wooden recalled in 2004. "He was giving an exhibition on ball handling and whatnot while advertising the shoe. I got to know him personally many years later. I would say it was primarily his ball handling and passing of the basketball. It was eye-opening and revolutionary to see a guy do that."

Wooden must be considered the first among equals in this class of early Indiana basketball pioneers, but Chuck Taylor belongs. Chuck achieved his glory not on the hardwood court, though he was a good industrial league player in the 1920s, and not in the coaching ranks, though he was the surprisingly successful head coach of an important Army Air Force service team during World War II. Nor was he a strategist, even though he published newspaper articles on the game and penned a "Fundamentals of Basketball" handbook that was widely distributed from the 1930s through the 1950s. Chuck Taylor did not invent or innovate anything truly important related to the game of basketball. What he invented was himself. He was both Barnum and Bailey to basketball; he was Houdini, and his greatest trick was in escaping his own modest athletic background and becoming the one and only "Chuck Taylor." In so doing he brought along millions of Americans with him in his love of the game.

Like many basketball stories, the Chuck Taylor saga begins in the heartland, in a part of southern Indiana so rural folks still call it "Kentuckiana," and in small Indiana towns called Azalia and Columbus. Only two weeks prior to his death in 1969, Chuck was to write about his humble origins. "There was a time when you didn't say you were born in Brown County, Indiana if you could help it, but now it's a very beautiful state park and it's the place the artists go to paint the leaves and the hills. That's where I was born. . . . I was born in the country—I think the nearest town was Nashville."[1]

Charles Hollis "Chuck" Taylor was born on June 24, 1901. That's what it says on Taylor's passport, which survives at Converse, Inc. headquarters in North Andover, Massachusetts. Authorities in Nashville, the Brown County seat, don't have a record of Chuck's birth, but records exist for his older brother, Howard E. Taylor, and for his kid sister, Elsie Taylor Breeding. Chuck's schoolteacher dad, James A. Taylor, was from Brown County for sure (born 1870), and his mother, the former Aurilla Cochran, was from Kansas.

Brown County might as well be in Appalachia. The tallest peaks in Indiana are in Brown County, and much of the greatest poverty in the state in the early part of the twentieth century was in the southern part of the county. Misty mornings over the substantial, tree-lined hills are highly reminiscent of the Great Smoky Mountains, and only the tourist trade and artists' colony in and near Nashville, plus the Brown County State Park, brought a modicum of prosperity to the area by the middle and latter part of the twentieth century. T. C. Steele, the most famous of the Hoosier landscape artists, painted near Nashville in Brown County, and legendary bluegrass artist Bill Monroe operated his music festival just up the road a few miles on Indiana 135 in Beanblossom for many years.

Older brother Howard was born in Brown County (no town listed) in 1893, and Elsie was born in 1907 in tiny Azalia in neighboring Bartholomew County, so Chuck's formative years were spent in Bartholomew County, in Azalia and Columbus.

Azalia was plotted in 1831. The town had sixty-four plots, each 264 feet square, and the population has never exceeded 200. The surrounding countryside probably looked much as it does today—densely forested woodland, save for a few clearings with cornfields and even a tobacco field right on the southern edge of the tiny town. Communications were poor in the mid-nineteenth century—a flat-bottom boat would take travelers down to Louisville, and travel elsewhere was by coach. Today, a historical marker confirms that Azalia was a real stop along the Underground Railroad during the Civil War era, and several newspaper articles over the years retold the story of escaped slaves who were helped on their way to Richmond, Indiana, near the Ohio border in the east central part of the state and home to Earlham College, the main higher educational institution of the Society of Friends in America. From Richmond they often continued north to Canada. Chuck Taylor would later make his own journey to Richmond, though for a far different purpose.

A Quaker meeting house from the late 1800s survives, as does the Little and Newsom General Store, which once housed the Bank of Azalia in a single vault on the main floor; they are at opposite ends of a small park in the center of town. The general store was long ago converted to apartments, but the country church still is active.

The brick Azalia Friends Meeting House suffered a devastating fire in 1998. Church member Larry Perkinson, a local schoolteacher, was painting the main chapel one Saturday afternoon late in 2003 when a stranger pulled into the gravel parking lot in front looking for bits and pieces of Chuck Taylor's life. The front door to the church was propped open, so the stranger went in. Chuck Taylor was remembered in Azalia, Perkinson said.

"The schoolhouse he would have attended was right where the parsonage is now," said Perkinson, "but the school building no longer is there."

A new, two-story brick school building was established at the north end of town in 1924, and records show that Chuck's dad was one of the first teachers there. The squarish, industrial-looking building closed circa 1962 and has been for sale for decades, with the shrubs and weeds now reaching almost to the roof, obscuring much of the façade. Other vestiges of the past, including a commuter rail bed that would have taken local residents north to Columbus and Indianapolis, can still be discerned. The rail bed disappears into a small cornfield just south of the township park. Another, more well defined rail bed runs through a thicket of trees and parallel to a nearby two-lane highway to the east of town, but the rails and ties were pulled up years ago. The mostly gravel driveways in Azalia now accommodate pickup trucks and people who commute to Columbus or Seymour for work, and about eighty families from throughout the region keep the Quaker church alive.

But Azalia—primitive, obscure, simple—was a place where a boy could be alone in the afternoons and bounce a leather-covered basketball on hard-packed dirt or practice a two-handed shot at an improvised goal for hours, and hone his skills and deepen his love for a new, growing game that would take him so very far in life.

Chuck likely graduated from the elementary school in Azalia where his dad taught, but the town never had a high school. So when Chuck was ready for the ninth grade—coming from a professional family he would not have been expected to farm or look for work in a factory after elementary school—his dad sent him up to Columbus to stay with George W. Taylor, Chuck's uncle and a baggage master for the Pennsylvania Rail Road. It was in the more urbane Columbus that Chuck first got a taste of organized ball and real competition.

Columbus, Indiana was a prosperous town of about 9,000 in the second decade of the twentieth century. It benefited from being the Bartholomew County seat as well as a manufacturing town and regional agricultural center. Two rail lines and an electric interurban commuter line crisscrossed the city. Besides manufactured goods and other items from a local tannery, the rail lines shipped cantaloupes, cucumbers, and tomatoes all the way to Indianapolis and beyond.[2]

This was a time in the still young American republic's life that many cities, great and small, fancied themselves the new Rome, and Columbus was no exception. A Romanesque-style red brick City Hall and tower were erected circa 1893, and still stand. Columbus also featured electric trolley cars in the early twentieth century, impressive for a town its size, as well as a pure water filtration plant. The swank Hotel St. Denis, complete with front portico and balcony, housed the city's leading restaurant, and many other substantial businesses downtown bespoke prosperity. Even to this day, with a population of no more than 39,000, ambitious Columbus features buildings by Eliel and Eero Saarinen, I. M. Pei, Robert Venturi, and other famous architects.

The high school shared in this prosperity. In 1917, a full-page ad from a local clothing store placed in *The Log*, the high school yearbook, featured a woodcut of a smartly dressed young man looking out over a patio, very Gatsby-like, while the text declared: "Two Very Important Facts for Young Men About This Store: One is, that we believe in young men; the other is, that they believe in us. It's a great combination. It has brought us the trade of the best dressed young men of Columbus. Right now they are strong for these new Hart Schaffner & Marx Varsity Fifty-Five Suits."[3]

Chuck only shows up in a couple of pictures in the yearbook, including as a member of the school's Athletic Association. Like all the other boys, he's shown on the front steps to the school, between two fluted pillars that appear to hold up the portico, and all are dressed in dark suits and ties. The girls generally are shown wearing dark skirts with white blouses, topped by sailor collars and small scarves tied around their necks and knotted in front. It's all a period piece, but they are prosperous, prosperous, prosperous. Even the student events throughout the school year listed in the yearbook bespoke what used to be called "breeding," or at least a striving for culture. The Dramatic Club staged "Green Stockings" by A. E. W. Mason, a comedy in three acts, and other plays; and the young "junior women" of the school held their annual reception in a hall "which was daintily adorned with pennants, ferns and flowers . . . while pillows and rugs added further to the charm and attractiveness of the scene," according to a report in *The Log*.[4]

The high school itself almost was a finishing school for the middle-class youth in town, those who did not have to go work in the local factories or tannery or fields. James A. Taylor may have wanted this good breeding for his son, something he never could have obtained in Brown County or in southern Bartholomew County, which weren't even electrified yet. And Chuck may have been influenced by his young peers—in later years he became a sharp dresser and stayed at fine hotels on his many road trips, and he moved up from second-class rail cars to Fords to Chevrolets to Lincoln Continentals in his personal stable of automobiles. Yet he was really identified with only one activity throughout all the pages of *The Log*, in every surviving *Log* for every year he attended Columbus High School. That was basketball.

Chuck proved to be a mainstay on the Columbus High School Bull Dogs from his first day at the school, quickly finding a spot on the freshman team during the 1915–16 school year. Yet it was during the season of 1918–19, when he was just seventeen and captain of the team, that he and his mates made their true mark. The Bull Dogs went all the way to the State High School Athletic Association single-class boys basketball finals in West Lafayette that year, and along the way Chuck was to personally bump up against young men like Wells and Vandivier, future Hall of Famers like himself.

The Bull Dogs had been touted in the pre-season as one of the favorites to win the boys basketball tournament, an annual event in the state since 1911 that drew about 400 teams and more than 4,000 players each March in its early years, inclusive of sectional and regional play.[5] The popularity of the tournament—one of the very first of its kind in the country—was a testament to the success of basketball generally in the state. When Alonzo Stagg, the famous University of Chicago football coach in the 1920s, hosted a boys high school basketball tournament for Illinois teams as well as those from surrounding states, he specifically barred all Indiana varsity squads, but would only allow "second teams" or "reserve teams" from the Hoosier state in the competition—that's how strong Indiana basketball was at the time.[6] Even into the twenty-first century, nine of the ten largest high school gyms in America, in terms of seating capacity, were in Indiana.[7]

Taylor was a healthy-looking lad during his high school

playing days. A surviving snapshot, taken in the spring or summer during the late teens in Columbus, shows him standing outside a hardware and sporting goods store with older brother Howard and younger sister Elsie, so prim in a frilly chiffon dress. Chuck is in shirt sleeves and he's overtly pugnacious, with an intense gaze focused directly on the camera lens and his long jaw jutting out prominently. He held his own on the court, too, as his high school yearbook reported during his sophomore year.

"Captain Charlie played guard, but he could also throw goals. He was good-natured and was never known to hit his opponent until that person hit him first. Class of Nineteen," declared a caption underneath a team photograph in the 1916–17 Log.[8]

The yearbook picture shows a clutch of eight staunch basketball players with a stylized letter C embroidered on their knit jerseys, not unlike the Cincinnati Reds' "C" of today. Taylor is seated with arms folded on the lower left in the group portrait. Coach Fred Busenberg, in a heavy wool suit and high, stiff collar, is seated in the middle of his boys. The uniform colors are not apparent in the monochrome photo, but other historical references note that the Bull Dogs wore blue and white togs.

Charlie—he was years away from reinventing himself as "Chuck" Taylor—had his dark, thick hair combed straight back and cropped close on the sides, almost a John Dillinger style, and it was a look he was to maintain at least through the mid-1920s, when he began thinning on top. He smiles sublimely in this photo—not cocky, not quite a smirk, but a surpassing smile nonetheless.

Hoops had arrived in Indiana in 1894—the first scheduled game was held at a YMCA in Crawfordsville on March 16, 1894, and the first intercollegiate game in America (between

Wabash College and Purdue) allegedly was held in the west central Indiana town the same year.[9] Basketball proved wildly popular in the state, yet high school teams that adopted the sport often played in makeshift venues, such as "the Rat Hole" in Westfield, north of Indianapolis, which had a ceiling so low there was only two feet of clearance above the rim.[10] Boys in Madison played on a local skating rink, and patrons were encouraged to come down to the court and put on their roller skates during halftime. Games in Carmel were played at a lumberyard—fans found seats on the stacks of wood.[11]

The Bull Dogs fared better than most. Columbus was proud of its high school basketball players. The school had no gymnasium, so the boys played their home games in the finest building in town, City Hall. The large, open room on the second level had a coffered tin ceiling about eighteen feet above the floor and enough space for more than 200 spectators squeezed along the sidelines. City Hall has been preserved and is now the Columbus Inn. The natural tile floor on the main level still features a geometric pattern with delicate pastel coloring, and the best suite in the house is on the second floor, up a wide stairway with a sweeping right turn, in a subdivided portion of what was the second-floor auditorium and gymnasium in the original floor plan.

The start of the 1918–19 basketball season was full of hope and self-confidence for the Bull Dogs. A preview in an Indianapolis newspaper said, "Columbus has the best prospects for a whirlwind winning team in the history of the school," and singled out two stars for special attention—senior "Charlie Taylor," the savvy team captain and a substantial playmaker on the court, and Erwin Gerhardt, a towering 6-foot-8 transfer student from Rockford, Illinois.[12]

The first contest of the 1918–19 season, Taylor's last as

a student and the high school's best up to that point, was an away game against the larger Arsenal Tech High School in Indianapolis, a public high school that still stands in a largely working-class neighborhood on the near east side of the city. The date was December 13, 1918, and a headline in the now defunct *Columbus Herald* told the story: "Tech No Match For Local Five: Columbus Shows Rare Form in First Game, Winning 23 to 12: Taylor Chief Score Maker for Columbus—Gerhart [*sic*] At Center Scores Points."[13]

The story overflowed with detail, which was unusual in basketball coverage at any level prior to the 1940s, and gushed with pride over the Bull Dogs' victory. Taylor had scored ten points in the contest, a good start to what would turn out to be a great season for the young player, and it's easy to imagine the ride home from Indianapolis to Columbus after the game, probably via coach on one of Indiana's good rail lines of the day. Taylor, already so purposeful in life, would not have been shy about accepting the plaudits of the press. Looking out the large picture window on the train car and into the snow-covered cornfields and wind breaks in December as they flashed by, he could feed on his own reflection in the glass and dream about more glory to come.

The Bull Dogs continued to post victories like crocuses popping up through the snow, and by February the early season predictions looked better than ever. "Edinburg Was Easy Picking For Locals: Latter Defeated Former by Score of 65 to 13 Here Last Night," read a newspaper headline on February 1, 1919, a Saturday.[14] Then, as now, high school athletics were a must-see on Friday nights in towns and cities across Indiana. Sixty-five points were a lot for a high school game in 1919. Edinburg, a smaller town between Columbus and Indianapolis, had only 2,000 or so citizens in those days, so Columbus was the giant in their cabbage patch. But Columbus had a good team by any standards; they were en route to the state finals in March.

The next Friday night Columbus won again, this time against highly regarded Franklin High School. The Franklin starters, who were to claim consecutive state tournament titles in 1920, 1921, and 1922, would eventually earn the accolade "The Wonder Five," both for their high school exploits and as members of the Franklin College team, where most continued their play. The most important player that evening for Franklin was "Fuzzy" Vandivier, and Taylor played opposite him at the forward position. It was a rare high school matchup of future Hall of Famers, and Taylor easily bested the younger Vandivier, outscoring him five points to none.[15]

The Bull Dogs ran their record to 11-1 that night, and the venue was Columbus City Hall, as usual for home games. The town's semi-pro team—the Columbus Commercials— also played a basketball game that evening, but the Bull Dogs of Columbus High School received top billing in the newspaper.

Next week, more of the same. "Captain Charlie Taylor tossed a ringer within 4 seconds of the start, and he followed it with another before the minute was over."[16] Though Columbus lost a rematch with Franklin, the Bull Dogs soon recovered, "walloping" Bedford 53-14 later in the month. Taylor scored seven points on three field goals and a foul shot, and Gerhardt had thirty-four points on seventeen baskets, an astonishing sum for a single player against a competitive team in those days.[17]

The Franklin games were noteworthy because they attracted gambling, an ever-present threat in any arena when someone wins and someone loses. Chuck first learned his trick passes and long field goal shots in Columbus, and he also learned about betting on games there. Though neither he nor any of his mates were implicated, the March 7, 1919 *Evening Republican* quoted the local police chief as saying no betting of any kind would be tolerated during the upcoming sectionals as had been reported during both Columbus-Franklin matchups. Those caught would be arrested and prosecuted, he fulminated.[18]

It was all basketball coverage in the Columbus papers now. "North Vernon Was Only Practice For Bull Dogs," declared a gleeful headline on March 8, referring to the opening match of the sectionals. Hundreds of students had paraded down city streets in support of their Bull Dogs, and the fire chief, who was in attendance at the game, personally turned many fans away for fear of overcrowding at the City Hall venue.[19] The Bull Dogs dominated in their Friday night opening tiff 40-8 and easily outpaced their next three opponents in morning, afternoon, and night games on Saturday to become sectional champions. They were a juggernaut.[20]

In an addendum to the history of these sectional games, the *Evening Republican* picked a "First Team" from among all the schools that participated. Taylor made first team, as did Gerhardt, certainly. But the honor was diluted for each young man because every first team member selected came from the Bull Dogs—the hometown newspaper simply picked the Columbus starters *en masse* for the first team.[21]

The Bull Dogs truly were strong, though. Newspaper accounts marveled at Gerhardt's dominance in the middle, but they also pointed to Taylor's court leadership and all-around skill. He was not a selfish player and there was no disparagement of his occasionally modest point totals (he was never more than third-leading scorer during any of his years in high school). A well-known referee complimented all the Columbus boys on their sportsmanship. "[T]he Columbus boys have one trait that will stand them in good stead at Purdue and that is that no matter what kind of scrap they get into, how hard they fall or how unfair a decision seems, they always come up smiling," said the man, identified only as referee Rathbun. "I sure expect to hear great things of Columbus in the state tourney."[22]

Indiana's State High School Athletic Association basketball tournament was famous for decades for its single-class competition, meaning all schools, large and small, played against each other for a single official state championship. The popular 1986 film *Hoosiers,* starring Gene Hackman, was based on the true story of Milan (pronounced MY-lan), a southern Indiana high school with a total enrollment of 161 that won the state championship in 1954, defeating future Hall of Famer Oscar Robertson and his teammates from Crispus Attucks High School in Indianapolis along the way and beating perennial powerhouse Muncie Central High School in the finals. The state tourney in 1919 was held at the Purdue University gym in West Lafayette, a leafy town on the banks of the Wabash River. (The previous year it had been held in Bloomington, home of Indiana University.) The big state colleges were top choices for the tournament because they had proper basketball arenas and seating for thousands to watch the contests. They usually filled the stands too.

The competition began well for Columbus on Friday, March 14. They simply buried South Bend 24-3. Gerhardt scored ten points on five goals, as did starting forward Crim. But the other forward, Taylor, scored none.[23] Columbus won its next game, played later that evening against the northeast Indiana town of Rochester, by a score of 11-5.

But it was not to be the Bull Dogs' year, and the disappointment in a failed championship bid was to be but the first in a series of near-misses that plagued Chuck Taylor's basketball career. In the quarterfinals, two-time former state champion Thorntown beat them 20-16.[24] "Result of Contest In Doubt Until the End," proclaimed the hometown newspaper, which would not be immune to the charge of boosterism. Gerhardt led the Bull Dogs with twelve points, and Taylor scored the other four. Bloomington High School (coached by Wells) would go on to win the state championship later in the evening, defeating Franklin in the finals. And it was to be Gerhardt, not Taylor, who was named to the tourney's All-Star team from the Bull Dogs' roster.[25]

No matter—Columbus was proud of its boys, and the city feted the team on Tuesday evening, March 18, in a banquet at the Tea Room, a local landmark, followed by yet another candlelit parade through downtown streets that again attracted hundreds. It was a crisp night with light flurries, so typical of Columbus winters, and speeches by Mayor Frank S. Jones, banker William G. Irwin, high school principal Donald DuShane, and Coach Busenberg were scheduled after the parade at the Bull Dogs' usual lair, City Hall itself.

"Three hurrahs, a couple of whoops and lots of other yell fandangles for the Columbus high school basketball players," declared a picturesquely worded newspaper editorial.[26] One City Hall speaker noted that Coach Busenberg received no compensation in his role as basketball coach, but only for his regular teaching duties at the school, and that each player on the team had passing grades in all subjects, which "exceeded" athletic association requirements of the day. In an emotional moment, Mayor Jones criticized the people of northern Indiana, who allegedly "didn't think very much of the people living in the southern half, and that the truth of the matter was that the southern half produced good men as well as good basketball players."[27] As always, it was the Kentuckiana issue.

Chuck Taylor was at the celebrations too. As the son of

a public school teacher, he could have been expected to go to college after graduation. Plus, college hoops had more status than professional basketball in those days. He'd play ball, get an education, perhaps become a high school teacher and basketball coach himself. But his mind was on other things. For in the same edition of the *Evening Republican* that summarized the Bull Dogs' banquet, there appeared a three-column-wide advertisement for a professional basketball game to be played that night, in the same auditorium in the same City Hall where the Bull Dogs had played all their home games.

"Basketball City Hall Wednesday Mch. 19: Columbus Commercials vs. Camp Grant Team: Can the Commercials come back? Come and see: Game Called at 8:15 p.m., Admission 25c."

The Columbus Commercials would be considered a semi-pro team today, as would most "professional" basketball teams in the first years of the sport's emerging popularity in America. The Commercials were sponsored by a businessmen's group, essentially a local chamber of commerce. They challenged teams from surrounding communities and occasionally clashed with so-called barnstorming teams of the era, which were either true pro teams that derived their revenues exclusively from roundball or were well-packed traveling teams sponsored by sporting goods manufacturers and retailers as a marketing tool. The Commercials played their home games at City Hall—it was the only suitable venue in town.

Young Taylor's mind was on the Commercials during the city's tribute to the Bull Dogs. This is known because Charles Hollis "Chuck" Taylor made his professional basketball debut on March 19, 1919, in that very game against the Camp Grant Five. While still in high school, while just seventeen years old and only a day after he and his mates were feted for going all the way to the state finals, Chuck Taylor played in his first pro contest. The game summary the next day showed that the Commercials beat the soldiers 45-30, but the only news that mattered to history revealed that "Taylor was substituted for Smith in the last three minutes of the game."[28]

As Taylor did not score any points in the contest, and the Columbus Commercials disbanded after the following season, it may seem like an inauspicious beginning to a professional basketball career. But who else from the 1919 sectional champion Columbus High School Bull Dogs and the Columbus Commercials semi-pro basketball team is remembered today?

Hall of Fame

Non-Skids

Charlie Taylor, at 6-foot-1 and 190 pounds, was becoming a man. His great shock of thick, dark hair was combed provocatively straight back over his head, and his long jaw demanded attention. He was just nineteen when he stepped forward with firm posture and resolute gait onto the floor of the Akron Firestone Clubhouse, "a dinky bandbox" of a gymnasium,[1] as one basketball player of the era called it, but an important landmark throughout the Midwest nonetheless. Less than two years out of high school, Taylor had done the unthinkable in pursuing a professional basketball career when such a thing hardly existed in America. By way of analogy, think of heading to Broadway before there *was* a Broadway. Chuck's career with the Commercials was short-lived, as the team folded the season following his graduation. He next likely played for two small-time Indianapolis teams, the Habichs and Omar Bakery, but Akron was his first true foray away from home. The most famous picture of Chuck in existence reveals how proud he was to be in this city, and to play for this team—it's 1921, and he's standing on the roof of the Firestone Tire and Rubber Company while wearing his heavy cotton duck shorts and a wool-fiber jersey with the antique Firestone "F" lettering on the chest.

Chuck was consumed by a vision of himself in basketball togs playing in front of packed stands in gymnasiums and fieldhouses everywhere. Well-known Indiana teams, such as the Fort Wayne Knights of Columbus and Indianapolis Kautskys, the latter owned by a local grocery store owner, were occasionally covered in Hoosier newspapers, as was the emerging great traveling team of the era, the New York City–based Original Celtics. Chuck's new team, the Akron Firestone Non-Skids, named for the leading brand of tire the famous company sold, was one of the most important teams in the early history of basketball in America. Technically an "industrial league" team, the Non-Skids nevertheless were serious about their sport. The team had recruited another Indiana legend, coach Paul "Pep" Sheeks from all-male Wabash College in Crawfordsville, Indiana, the year before Chuck's arrival, and the Non-Skids were a founding member of the National Basketball League in 1937. It was that league that merged in 1949 with the Basketball Association of America to become the NBA as it is known today. All the Non-Skids had jobs during the day at the factory, a practice that continued at most industrial league teams for years, but Chuck really was in town for one purpose, and that was to score points on the hardwood floor.

Basketball in general was taking root in America. Most

colleges had varsity teams by this time, and early pro circuits, such as the Eastern League, with teams from Trenton, Newark, Philadelphia, Scranton, and elsewhere, clamored for attention. Yet pay was erratic, often just a few dollars per game, and players often jumped from one team to another during a season, or even played on different rosters during the same season. Pro basketball was followed by a hardy cadre in the public, and, as with football, college hoops was far more popular and respectable in the public eye. Still, metropolitan newspapers occasionally would publish little blurbs about upcoming pro contests, or print a final score, but usually with few details of the actual play.

America was an emerging powerhouse on the world stage in 1921. The Great War (the war to end all wars, a war fought to make the world safe for democracy, President Woodrow Wilson had declared) was over, and the prosperity inherent in the roaring '20s had begun. A well-developed intercity rail system and the rise of the automobile meant players could reach new audiences quickly and cheaply. Opportunity existed as never before, and horizons were expanding. The country's population stood at close to 120 million and the character of the nation was changing from agrarian to industrial capitalism. This meant something for sport as well. Whereas the very earliest professional basketball teams typically grew out of settlement houses or YMCAs (such as the "Olympic champion" Buffalo Germans, named for a German Street YMCA in Buffalo, New York in the 1890s) or were traveling sideshows managed by sketchy promoters that went from town to town scaring up a game where they could, a new generation of teams was being sponsored by large factories and industrial concerns that had some staying power and real clout. Besides Firestone, the Goodyear Company also sponsored a team in Akron called the Wingfoots (and they made a rubber-soled, canvas, high-top athletic shoe of their own also called the Wingfoot). General Electric sponsored an important team in Fort Wayne, Indiana about this time. In fact, the Wingfoots and G.E. Techs were co–founding members with the Non-Skids of the National Basketball League in 1937.

A growing middle class and skilled labor force were gravitating to basketball. The game often was played in dance halls, often as an added attraction for paying customers before a flapper dance or jazz concert. The Harlem Globetrotters, for example, started life as the Savoy Big Five in 1926—the team was named after a South Side Chicago ballroom where it originally played its games as part of a double bill with local bands. More informally, basketball caught fire with eastern European immigrants in the urban slums, in part because it was cheap to equip a team and the game could be played in a back alley or the friendlier confines of a neighborhood settlement house.

Basketball was scrappy in those days, and Chuck was to recall the ferocity of play at the professional level in an interview years later. "When I first broke in, the double dribble was legal," he said. "There were no backboards for the baskets. The ball had to be there for sure. They also used nets all the way around the court. When the nets were closed for the game it was like being in a cage. The difference now is that the courts are much better, there is better coaching, and the balls are rounder. However, you will have to convince me that the shooting is better."[2]

Indeed, this is an accurate picture of the sport in its infancy. Early court sizes were not standardized, and the game was played inside wood scaffolding bound by wire mesh or between screened curtains hanging from the rafters in the gymnasium or other venue, which led to the name "cage ball" as well as references to players as "cagers." The cages kept the ball in bounds longer for more continuous action on the court, but they also discouraged unruly fans from throwing objects at the players. Defense was rugged, too, with undisciplined man-to-man (*mano a mano,* basically) defenses with few fouls ever called, at least at the professional level—think roller derby today. For all their accumulated bruises from flying elbows and uncalled "charges," and road rash–type burns from sliding on the hardwood court, the athletes fortunate enough to play in an industrial league got a regular check from the factory paymaster on Friday evenings, while the players for the independents were paid perhaps $15 a game. It was into this exciting but uncertain world that young Charlie Taylor embarked on his basketball quest. He did well to land on his feet in Akron, in part because of the ongoing competition between crosstown rivals Firestone and Goodyear, and in part because it guaranteed young combatants a regular paycheck. "Firestone Tire & Rubber and Goodyear were the principal industries in Akron and arch-rivals in basketball," wrote basketball historian Robert W. Peterson. "Their players had jobs in the plants and were not paid extra for playing on the company team."[3] The Firestones lasted until 1941, though the league they helped found lasted longer, and the game the team helped pioneer seemingly will last forever. The Wingfoots fared better, continuing well into the 1960s as an Amateur Athletic Union powerhouse. Longtime NBA coach and University of North Carolina alumnus Larry Brown played for the Wingfoots in 1964, the year he was chosen for the U.S. Olympic squad.

Akron is part of the Cleveland megalopolis today, but it would have had its own identity in the 1920s. The factories, the smokestacks, the ethnic neighborhoods and cosmopolitanism of a mid-sized American city all would have contributed to Chuck's education. Life in Akron would have broadened his shoulders and imbued him with even more gumption than he already had, and it would have required him to hone his considerable interpersonal skills as much as his play on the court. He was away from Indiana for the first time, and like most young, unattached men of the era, he likely stayed in one of the many boardinghouses lining the side streets in the industrial part of the city. But he stayed in touch with his family back home. This is known because the first newspaper clippings in his mother's fabric-covered scrapbook, the old-fashioned kind tied with lacing up and down its spine, date from just this era.

Chuck broke into the Non-Skids' roster with a bang. "[I]t was Taylor's perfect basket fifteen seconds before the whistle that brought home the bacon," noted the Firestone company newsletter, itself called the *Non-Skid,* which profusely credited Taylor in a tight 28-26 victory over archrival Goodyear late that season.[4] The newsletter reproduced a montage of all the Non-Skids players, their busts plastered on the image of a roughly stitched basketball. "Taylor"—no first name as usual in sports reporting in those days, but it is Chuck, with his long face and brushed-back head of hair—was shown on the lower left. "Pep" Sheeks was featured in the center of the basketball.[5] Another player on the Firestones was "Neihaus," a Seymour, Indiana native who was to maintain a relationship with Taylor throughout the '20s. The game-winning basket with only seconds left to play was so electric, so indelible in local basketball lore that it was recalled decades later in a special newspaper supplement about the history of Akron basketball. In what was being hailed as the memorable 1921 season, the retrospective noted that "Firestone beat Goodyear twice—the second time on a shot two-thirds the length of the floor with two seconds left—to win the city industrial championship."[6] That was Taylor's shot, though the article, published in 1996, never makes the connection to the famous basketball shoe icon.

The sensational basket represented the only two points Taylor scored in the game, yet it apparently was enough to earn Chuck a spot in the starting rotation. "Taylor, Neihaus and Bonds did stellar work for the Firestone brigade," the factory newsletter soon was reporting after a later game.[7] Taylor was the second-highest scorer on his team that night with nine points. More importantly, he started at right forward, which was his natural position in high school. The always competitive Taylor seemed to have found a home.

Unstated in coverage at the time, but almost certainly true, was that Chuck Taylor introduced a quick passing game wherever he went. Chuck on the court always was a playmaker, passing the ball smartly, efficiently, almost invisibly. By the time his name became legend in the 1930s, commentators were crediting him with inventing the one-handed pass, and it's likely true. He was a good shooter but rarely the leading scorer on any of his teams. Rather, he knew how to find the leading scorer.

The Non-Skids played their home games in the Firestone Clubhouse, a "horrible place to play," a former Goodyear Wingfoot was to complain years later, but it was virtually a community center for the thousands of Firestone employees and their families who lived nearby. The clubhouse also hosted roller hockey games and was used for dances, too, including a "hop" at the end of the 1921 regular basketball season to honor the Non-Skids. Like period photographs, the language employed in the factory newsletter to promote the hop is a keepsake today. "Well, they certainly played rings around the other teams and that's why and how the Firestone quintet copped the championship of the Akron Industrial Basketball

League," the anonymous author gushed. "Excellent floor work and clever team play did the trick for the Firestone chaps."[8]

The 1920–21 season had been good enough to earn the Non-Skids a trip to the American Industrial Athletic Association national championship in Erie, Pennsylvania that year, a tournament that preceded the NCAA "Final Four" by twenty years. Twenty-six teams were invited to play in the tourney, to be held Thursday through Saturday, March 17–19, coinciding with a national convention and election of officers that attracted hundreds of business and industrial leaders to the northern Pennsylvania city.[9]

The importance of the American Industrial Athletic Association is all but forgotten today, but it was clearly inspired by both the recently revived Olympic ideal and the YMCA movement. The AIAA, which was mostly upper midwestern and northeastern in orientation, coinciding with the region of popularity for basketball, was founded circa 1919. It also had a clear political angle—to keep working men and women away from "red" organizations. News of the Bolshevik Revolution in Russia filled newspapers of the day, including the *Akron Beacon Journal,* which almost daily ran articles about "true Americanism" and the like. News pages across America were filled with allegations of communist infiltration and "red" labor organizers in the nation's factories and mines. Sport was an antidote to revolution.

During the March 1921 competition, for example, an Erie newspaper spoke of a full political program related to the convention, including several talks on the value of sports and recreation at industrial sites across the country.[10] William Burdick of Baltimore spoke on "Loyalty in Athletics" and cited the "true story" of an incorrigible reform-school inmate who later became a model citizen after joining an athletic program. The talk anticipated by several decades publication of Alan Sillitoe's *The Loneliness of the Long-Distance Runner,* a novel about an English prison inmate who is encouraged to run competitively as part of his rehabilitation. (In the novel, however, the incorrigible youth sabotages the warden's best efforts by intentionally losing a race, thereby rejecting liberal humanism and social reform imposed from above.)

The AIAA promoted all kinds of athletics for men and women, including basketball, track events, bowling, and "roller polo," which would look like hockey on roller skates today. Women's basketball games typically were played as warmups for the men's games, and this led to a controversy back in Akron as early as January 1920, the year prior to Chuck's arrival, when the women athletes demanded a share of gate receipts.[11]

Exact attendance figures for the 1921 games are not available, but more than 600 worker-athletes had come out for "workingman's play" during the 1920 games, which had been held in Akron.[12] It's likely the Erie event drew at least as many participants, in part because it was held closer to the populous East Coast, drawing teams from New York State and Massachusetts as well as from the Great Lakes region.

"Tonight will witness the opening of the A.I.A.A. basketball tournament, the first of its kind ever staged in this city, and seventeen of the best basketball aggregations boasted by shops the country over are scheduled to compete," declared an Erie newspaper on March 17, 1921.[13] Apparently not all twenty-six invited teams made it to the city, but no matter. On the card the first night were the G.E. Techs from Fort Wayne and the Akron Firestones. The newspaper listed the starting lineups a day ahead of the match and Taylor was not on the Akron list, but he shone in the contest once it was played. Taylor, at left forward that night, was high scorer on his team with eight points on four field goals to lead Akron to a 41-

25 whipping of the General Electric team. "The Akron team played one of the snappiest, most evenly balanced games ever seen in Erie, depending entirely on short passes and direct shots from within the basket circle for their points," touted an Erie reporter. "McFayden, Taylor and Bonds formed a combination that had the Techs completely outclassed."[14]

Alas, the Firestone aggregation bowed out in the next round, losing decisively to Carnegie Steel 43-29. Neither of the Erie papers nor the *Akron Beacon Journal* carried a box score of that game. If it was any consolation to the tire makers from Akron, Carnegie Steel was the ultimate victor in the tourney.

As in any championship, all but one team go home disappointed, nursing their wounded pride or perhaps celebrating a moral victory in having done better than expected. The Firestone Non-Skids did not grab the honors in Erie, but this was still the kind of championship season that always set a fire under young Taylor. His Columbus High School Bull Dogs did not win the state championship in 1919 either, but they came close. That whets an appetite more than an easy victory. The Non-Skids vied for a national championship in 1921, and this is what Taylor lived for. And he had come on strong near the end of the season in his personal play.

Yet Taylor's name does not appear on the Firestone roster the following season. The company also had a Firestone Bank team in another league, and Taylor didn't play for that one, either. The Akron press continued to cover the Non-Skids, of course, but it was coach Sheeks who was building a reputation for himself and garnering more and more attention. Sheeks was to coach the team for the next twenty years, in fact. After a couple of pre-season games during the 1921–22 season, it was clear Taylor had been replaced.

"Sheeks' new forward, Spencer, put up a good fighting

game," read one game summary.[15] Later box scores continued to tout Spencer, but there never was a mention of Taylor again. Perhaps he had been cut. Chuck was inordinately loyal to fellow Hoosiers throughout his life once he became famous, yet you won't find any additional references to coach Paul "Pep" Sheeks and Chuck Taylor on the same page following the 1920–21 Akron Firestone season.

3.

Salesman

Akron may have been a watershed in Chuck Taylor's playing days. Firestone and Goodyear basketball continued to prosper, but Chuck was not part of it. After leaving the Non-Skids, he moved to Detroit and joined teams supported by first the Dodge Brothers, the famous automobile manufacturers, then by the T. B. Rayl Company, a large sporting goods retailer in the city. What Chuck had learned in Akron, besides some pointers from Sheeks and skills gained in competitive play, was the art of self-promotion. The *Akron Beacon Journal* covered Firestone and Goodyear basketball well, and the local factory boys were treated like real stars. Chuck took a few newspaper clippings and that rooftop photo of him in a Firestone uniform and made himself out to be a celebrity when he arrived in Detroit. The game plan? Reinvent himself.

First, he wangled a small story in one of the Detroit papers in late 1921 after he joined the Dodge Brothers factory team. Taylor "is generally regarded here as the smartest handler of the ball seen in a local uniform in some years," the short item proclaimed, accompanied by that rooftop photo of Chuck in the Firestones' jersey.[1] The move to the Rayls was even more provident. The Rayls often traveled to other midwestern cities, including in Indiana and Wisconsin, and claimed a "Midwest championship" in 1919. They also made a couple of appearances in Fort Wayne, where Chuck might first have heard of them.[2] Chuck may have worked on the assembly line for Dodge during the day, and he most likely sold athletic goods for Rayl. As both company teams were sponsored, Chuck would have worked and/or played ball on salary—a security blanket that was to become increasingly important to him later in life.

The T. B. Rayl connection proved to be important in another way. As a large retail sporting goods store, it would have sold Converse All Star shoes, which had been introduced in 1917, as well as other popular court shoes of the era, such as those by Spalding, Goodyear, and others. Converse, a manufacturer with regional headquarters in Chicago, was a larger company than Rayl. It would have been a logical progression for the ambitious Taylor to move from the Motor City to the Windy City in 1922, after just one season, to work for Converse. That's just what he did. What's not certain, though, is whether Chuck played basketball for Converse as part of the move in 1922. There's no evidence Converse fielded a team in the early 1920s, though the evidence is clear that by 1926 Converse was sponsoring a traveling team. Yet Chuck probably did continue his basketball career in some significant fashion right away when he moved to Chicago. A 1940 article in the *Detroit News,* published on the occasion of a Chuck

Taylor clinic, quoted one source as saying Taylor was known in Detroit basketball circles in the old days and that he often went to Chicago on weekends to suit up for games with teams either based there or traveling through.[3]

Chuck Taylor started his career in sales with the Converse Rubber Shoe Company in 1922. It is this connection—moving inventory, not driving to the basket—that brought Chuck true fame in his life. Over time, there were to be many versions of how Chuck Taylor came to work for Converse. For example, the Taylor biography on hand at the Naismith Memorial Basketball Hall of Fame in Springfield, Massachusetts reports that Chuck "walked into Converse's Chicago sales office in the summer of 1921 complaining of sore feet and persuaded Converse executives, and company founder Marquis Converse, to create a shoe specifically for basketball."[4]

That's unlikely to be the case. The Converse Rubber Shoe Company was based in Malden, Massachusetts in those days, and Marquis Converse, a native New Englander and former department store owner, would not have worked in the Chicago regional office. Also, the Converse All Star already was in production as an all-purpose court shoe. Chuck's name was not added to the ankle patch until 1932, after his marketing genius became evident.

In later years, Chuck was to give his own equally suspect version of events. He gave an interview to *Cincinnati Post* columnist Pat Harmon that was recalled in 1969. Harmon asked Chuck, who was by then old, balding, and overweight, how he got into the shoe business. It was all because of Nat Holman, Chuck replied, referring to the famous Original Celtics player and later basketball coach at City College of New York. It was at the height of the Celtics' fame, some forty years earlier, and Holman allegedly had received a letter from the Converse Rubber Shoe Company. "It's from some shoe company offering me $50 a month to walk into sporting goods stores and mention a good word for their shoes," Nat told Chuck. Nat wouldn't do it, but Chuck mulled the offer, then accepted on his own.[5]

The year of the offer allegedly was 1921, and within a year, Chuck claimed, he was on the road selling shoes and delivering the first of his famous basketball clinics.

Converse, founded in 1908, was a company that relied almost exclusively on its own sales force to sell shoes in its first decades. Marquis Converse despised jobbers and middlemen, who would cut into his profits and perhaps not be loyal to his product, so he formed a nationwide sales force that would call on independent retailers directly.[6] That's the real job Chuck took with the company initially.

Chuck was a terrible salesman at first. His widow was to recall in a 1979 interview that the young man from Columbus, Indiana had to be taught the basics of assertiveness by another famous Indiana-based sports legend. "It was a man-to-man, arms-around-the-shoulders talk by Knute Rockne that really kicked Chuck's sales career into high gear," Lucy Taylor Hennessey said. The year was 1922 and Chuck was in South Bend for a sales call with the fabled Notre Dame coach; Indiana was his first sales territory.

"He walked around the gym because he was afraid to go in, until finally Mr. Rockne came out and said, 'Son, what do you want?' And they got to be friends," his widow reported.[7] Rockne, the inspirational speaker who died in an airplane crash in mid-career, told Chuck to stiffen his spine, look men straight in the eye, and stretch out his hand toward them in friendship without hesitation.

This was the kind of paternal lecture young Taylor needed. Chuck was independent-minded during his Columbus days.

There's no evidence he hated his father—on the contrary, he was to bring his father James and older brother Howard into several business sidelines he started in the 1930s. But he listened to Knute Rockne.

Chuck's earliest sales technique will be familiar to neophyte salesmen everywhere—he simply called on people he knew, chewed the fat, and counted on them to help a fellow Hoosier. For example, Clifford Wells, by then an executive at the Naismith Memorial Basketball Hall of Fame Museum, claimed in a eulogy shortly after Chuck's death that he was one of Taylor's first customers.[8] In time, so were most of Indiana's coaches, including Everett Dean, the longtime Indiana University basketball coach, and Everett Case, the North Carolina State basketball coach who also coached at several Indiana high schools in the '20s and '30s, including Taylor's alma mater for a brief period.

Eventually Chuck became the consummate salesman. Surviving business associates say he was a great listener and would relay suggestions for improvements to the shoe (more padding under the ball of the foot, different rubber compound in the sole for less marking, and so on) to his regional office, and he'd always see to it that special orders were filled, even if that meant shoes had to be custom-sewed or modified at increased cost to the company.[9]

"Charlie would say 'I have this order [from a high school or college team], but I'm not going to give it to you [an independent retailer] unless you take our shoe and put it in the window'," recalled Bob Houbregs, a former Fort Wayne Piston and longtime Converse executive. "That's how he got a lot of sales."

Retired UCLA coach John Wooden became another loyal customer. He wore the shoe in high school in Martinsville, Indiana in the mid-1920s, and later in college at Purdue University, before Chuck's name was added to the ankle patch. Wooden also wore them while playing early pro ball for the Indianapolis Kautskys. His high school players in South Bend, Indiana wore them in the 1930s. But one year the South Bend cagers donned another shoe. At the insistence of a school board member, Wooden outfitted his young players with the similar Ball-Band shoe, a rubber-soled, high-top canvas competitor that was made in nearby Mishawaka, Indiana. "I think he was a stock holder in the Ball-Band. In fact, I know he was," Wooden recalled. "I switched to them one year. In one of the games we were playing one of the players came down the floor and made a quick stop and turn and the whole sole of one shoe practically came off. It was just hanging from the back. Just his sock foot was on the floor. I went back to the Converse shoe regardless of the board member."

Chuck filled in details of his sales technique in the Pat Harmon interview cited above. "I'd show up at a college or high school with a sample case and a reputation as a pro basketball player," Taylor continued. "The coach would ask me to put on a suit and show his players some of my tricks. That got to be a regular routine. Then one day I was scrimmaging with the team at North Carolina State. The coach asked me if I'd also say a few words to the players. I gave a short talk. I put the demonstration and the ball together, got some pointers on showmanship from Knute Rockne and went on the road full-time. I quit the Celtics and went around the world giving Chuck Taylor basketball clinics."[10]

Chuck indeed made calls on high school and college coaches, and he likely would have given pointers to the boys on how to play the game. Basketball was growing in popularity in the 1920s, but most coaches still were the football or baseball coaches who were given charge of the cage team during their off-seasons, and the rules of the game still were chaotic, with different rules for professional, Amateur Athletic Union, YMCA, and regional play. A Johnny Appleseed of the game would have been welcome, and Converse was to create a long tradition of hiring former players to put on clinics after Chuck's career began to wane in the 1950s.

Yet part of Chuck's interview with Harmon clearly reveals a new, alarming trend in the Chuck Taylor story. He may have been a veteran pro basketball player, but in no way was he authentically associated with legendary pre-modern teams such as the "world champion" Original Celtics and "Olympic champion" Buffalo Germans, both of which were repeatedly associated with Chuck's name over the years. The Original Celtics, founded by promoter Jim Furey in 1918, were a true barnstorming team that traveled the country beating up on local heroes and small-town teams. Future Hall of Famer Henry "Dutch" Dehnert led the 1918 iteration to a 65-4 record in its first year and was a mainstay of the team throughout its existence. During the 1922–23 season the team was credited with a 204-11 won-lost record, and the Celtics regularly drew 4,000 or more to its home arena, the Central Opera House in New York. Nat Holman joined the team in 1921. Joe Lapchick, yet another Hall of Famer, also played for the team in the 1920s.[11]

Chuck Taylor never played for that great team, however. "I can guarantee you Chuck Taylor never played for the Celtics," said author Murry Nelson, who collected every single permanent roster from the team for his 1999 biography of the Celtics—Chuck Taylor's name is nowhere to be found.[12]

Longtime Converse executive and former basketball great Grady Lewis also disputes that Taylor ever played with the Celtics. "He may have drunk a cup of tea with the Celtics," but that's all, Lewis said.

Chuck didn't stop with the Celtics, either. The other great

pre–modern era team that he's also associated with was the Buffalo Germans, which like the Original Celtics is in the Hall of Fame as a team. The Germans' fame as America's great early team predates that of the Celtics. The team was named the Germans after the German Street YMCA, where they were founded in 1895. "Over three seasons starting in 1908, led by star player Al Heerdt and coach Fred Burkhardt, the Germans won 111 straight games, defeating their opponents by more than 30 points a game," declares the Naismith Memorial Basketball Hall of Fame statement on the team. "The team disbanded in 1929 after having compiled a 792-86 record."[13]

The team was remembered by some in Buffalo because of its favorite venue, the Elmwood Music Hall at Elmwood and Virginia Streets. For many years the music hall featured an elaborate pipe organ that earlier had been featured in the Temple of Music built for the 1901 Pan-American Exposition there.[14]

Geoff Burgeson, a Buffalo resident and unofficial historian of the Buffalo Germans, says his grandfather, Ed Miller, was an original member of the Buffalo Germans in 1895, and his uncle, Harry Miller, joined the Germans in 1908. Burgeson has made a career of keeping the Germans' name alive. He says Taylor never played for that team, either.

"I have read through my files and find no reference to anyone with the last name 'Taylor' having an association with the Germans," Burgeson said. "I too am a little [skeptical] of the claim that Chuck Taylor played with the Germans. . . . Just the bare facts strike me as improbable—he strikes me as someone from a time and geography far removed from Buffalo."

The claims were all part of the persona Chuck was creating for himself as a "veteran" of these early pro teams. In later newspaper interviews, particularly from the 1930s and beyond, Chuck would invoke these teams, which still had a hold on the basketball public's imagination, sign an autograph or two, and sell shoes. Often the claims were contained in Converse handouts that were copied verbatim by local reporters when Chuck Taylor was making an appearance in town.

John Wooden said he knows all about the claims. He blames Converse, not Chuck, for spreading the myth. "I'm not sure Chuck would personally say that, but the company would say that about him," Wooden said. "It's just like one of the players that played basketball for me. He was an actor [Mike Connors]. He never got to play any. But as the years go on he just gets better and better. He [supposedly] played on a championship team, but the only problem is the years he played we didn't have a championship team."

Yet Chuck did play on one great team of the 1920s that was completely forgotten for decades, even by the company that sponsored it. The Converse Rubber Shoe Co., just like other large industrial concerns and sporting goods manufacturers and retailers, sponsored a basketball team called the All-Stars (spelled with the hyphen, unlike the shoe itself). The All-Stars, based in Chicago, were all about marketing the shoe. The drumbeat of ads nationally for the Converse All Star shoe meant the company needed to put a team on the road and reach the most dyed-in-the-wool basketball fans who would fill the stands to witness games in person. It's possible Chuck began playing for the All-Stars in 1922, when he moved to Chicago, but surviving evidence of the team's existence (a single yellowed newspaper photo and a couple of clippings) on hand at Converse headquarters dates only from the 1926–27 season.

The All-Stars were a great team, and Chuck was the player-manager during the 1926–27 season, when he toured with it across Indiana and other midwestern states. Sure, the idea was to sell shoes and demonstrate the product, but it was basketball. The kid who turned professional at age seventeen was still hanging in. And, in demonstrating the game and the shoe, he was continuing to put his name out there for the world to see.

"PRO CAGE FIVE TO TRAIN HERE: Converse Rubber Company's Team Will Work Out in Eagle Gym." That was the headline in the *Richmond* (Ind.) *Item* on Friday, October 8, 1926. "The Converse Rubber company's professional basketball team has signed to practice for the 1926 season in Richmond. . . . The Converse team will work out in the Eagle gym from October 25 until November 8, and will probably open in Richmond against the champion New York Celtic professional team in the early part of November."[15]

It was big news that a pro traveling team would hold its pre-season in Richmond, a town on U.S. 40 near the Ohio border. Frank Clark, from the Eastern League, was trumpeted as the fastest man on the squad. Carlyle Friddle, well-known to Hoosier basketball fans as one of the pillars of both the Franklin High School and Franklin College "Wonder Five" championship teams, also was touted—he'd be at center. F. Neihaus, who had played with Chuck five years earlier in Akron, was at guard. Chuck Taylor would be the player-coach.

"TAYLOR ARRIVES TO PUT CONVERSE SQUAD THROUGH WORK-OUTS." That was the bold headline a couple of weeks later. "Charles Taylor arrived in Richmond Monday with the first contingent of his all-star Converse basketball team that has to date, approximately 115 games booked for play during the 1926–27 season. Taylor has appeared in Richmond with the professional quintets in other years as a special man with the Ft. Wayne Knights of Columbus team when it played the New York Celtics."[16]

Why Taylor chose Richmond for his pre-season is not clear, but the Richmond newspapers of the day routinely advertised great rail connections to Chicago, where the Converse team was based. Both the C&O and Pennsylvania Railroad had daily sleeper cars to and from Chicago and Richmond.

Richmond is home to Earlham College, a leading Quaker institution, and was the home of Gennett Records, a popular label in the 1920s and 1930s. Gennett billed itself as the "birthplace of recorded jazz," and the label's artists included Hoagy Carmichael, Louis Armstrong, and Jelly Roll Morton, among others. The Old National Road, which was the first federal "highway" in America, passes right through town. The National Road carried culture as well as finished goods from the East, and even the architecture in Richmond is distinctly eastern, down to a well-preserved block of row houses near downtown that are highly reminiscent of Philadelphia row houses. And the wide, powerful Whitewater River passes through Richmond; high bluffs overlooking the river make for a dramatic view of the gorge below.

The town was basketball-crazy as well. The local newspapers covered all high school games in the city, as well as games in several surrounding communities. Richmond featured a local industrial league, and the Pennsylvania Railroad had its own six-team league. The city also had an entry in the semi-professional Central Indiana League. An all-girl team, the Kodaks, was sponsored by a camera store. They all were covered by the local press.

The facilities in town were attractive. The Richmond Athletic Association Coliseum, erected in 1902, had a brick façade and tall, peaked roof, plus a mezzanine that ran all the way around the court for seating and viewing. The coliseum was home to many high school and semi-pro basketball games in its early years, and it featured roller skating on nights when there was no game. It could seat about 2,000 people. The Eagle Gym, which belonged to a local chapter of the Fraternal Order of Eagles, was popular for boxing and wrestling matches and was available for rent, which is apparently what Chuck did.

The city also featured two well-established sporting goods companies, including the Ray B. Mowe Co. (the All-Stars scheduled at least one exhibition against the Mowe team) and The Geo. Brehm Co., which sponsored a team called "Brehm Plus Five," apparently because one of the owners (or his son) played on the squad.

The All-Stars started their pre-season in earnest in late October. In addition to Clark, Friddle, Neihaus, and Taylor, the team was joined by Joe Atherton from the important Washington (D.C.) Palace Laundry team and Sid Sankovic of Detroit. Six men were a common complement for a traveling team in those days—five starters and a player-coach.[17]

The All-Stars opened play with a "scrimmage" against Richmond's Central League entry on Friday evening, October 29, 1926. The exhibition had been touted in the press on several occasions prior to the game and no admission was charged. "The teams are not playing what could be branded a regulation basketball game—they merely are meeting for friendly competition for the betterment of the team play of each."[18] When the game finally was played, Taylor and Clark were at the forward position, Friddle was at center, and Atherton and Sankovic were at guard. But no score was recorded; it was just a scrimmage.[19]

The All-Stars took to the road on November 8 for a tour of many Indiana cities that fall and early winter. Games were played in Fort Wayne, Indianapolis, Seymour, Washington, Terre Haute, Evansville, and elsewhere, including at least one in Minneapolis, Minnesota. The Seymour game represented a quaint homecoming for Neihaus, Chuck's old friend from Akron, who the hometown newspaper dutifully announced would be "visiting his aunt, Miss Elizabeth Strodtman," while in the city.[20]

"One half of the game will be played under collegiate and the other half under professional rules," a second story on the Seymour game revealed. "Under the latter, the double dribble is permitted and there is no limit to the number of personal fouls as long as they are not accompanied by unnecessary roughness."[21] A follow-up story after the game noted that Converse had their way with the locals, downing them 41-23, and there was a bitter dispute over that double dribble rule during the second half.[22]

The Terre Haute newspaper covered the All-Stars' clash in a series of three articles in December, an unusual commitment of space at the time. Terre Haute, not far from the banks of the Wabash River, was more prominent in the first half of the twentieth century than after and had several of the state's first steel-skeleton high-rise buildings, even though its population always was far less than that of Indianapolis. Terre Haute was the original "crossroads of America" in Indiana because both U.S. 40 and U.S. 41 (the latter stretching from Chicago to Florida) passed through it. The town also was a main distribution center for bootleg liquor throughout the United States during the Prohibition era.

"Jensen Bros. Play Crack Court Crew: Twice State Champs Oppose Converse All Stars At Pennsy. Gym Thursday Night." That was the headline in the December 15, 1926 edition of the *Terre Haute Tribune*. "Led by Manager 'Duke' Lovell, the local quintet ranks with the best independent teams in the middle west. Lovell, ex-Garfield flash, will play one of the forward posts."[23]

The Converse team, "representative of the best independent teams in the middle west," was of the "first water," the *Tribune* declared. Clark and Friddle were counted as the true stars of the team, Sankovic and Neihaus both saw their names misspelled, and Taylor and Atherton rounded out the lineup. The game was promoted again on the day of the event, and the results were published the day after the contest, which spoke to the prominence of the event in the city. Friddle, starting at guard, scored nine points in the contest. Taylor, who started at forward, netted three. Yet the All-Stars lost the game—one of their rare losses that year.

No evidence of Chuck's role with the Converse All-Stars remains after the 1926–27 season. Chuck continued to promote himself, and his shoe, by making "special appearances" in which he would be installed into the starting lineup of a local team for an important match, such as when he earlier appeared with the well-known Fort Wayne Knights of Columbus team. An appearance with the Dayton (Ohio) Kellys in December 1927 was a superb example of this promotional tactic.

The obscure Kellys show up in a summary of professional basketball for the 1929–30 season, but they existed before this.[24] The team actually belonged to a Dayton municipal league, and was sponsored by Jim Kelly, Inc., a Dayton sporting goods store.[25] It was on December 17, 1927, that Taylor suited up with Kellys in a heavily promoted game against the "world champion" Original Celtics, a team Chuck clearly was obsessed with.

"Chuck Taylor, who is appearing with the Kellys tonight against the Celtics, is making a trip clear from the state of Mississippi for the game," a story announced on the day of the game. "Taylor is field representative for the Converse shoe company. He promised Jim Kelly recently that he would be on hand to play with his club if they met the Celtics, and he is making the long journey to keep his word with his friend."[26]

The story was a "plant," either by Kelly on his own, or at Taylor's instigation. Typically, local advertisers could expect a little free publicity for their promotions in the hometown newspaper, and this was a case in point. Chuck donned a pair of shorts and knee pads minutes before the game and, after the de rigueur introduction for the Converse salesman and "veteran" pro athlete from center court, he and the Kellys gave the Celtics a good run. "The score was 33 to 28 when the final whistle blew. No local club ever showed better passing against the Celts than did the Kellys, bolstered by Chuck Taylor. . . . Chuck Taylor toned up the Kellys' passwork to a high pitch."[27]

Chuck was doing well with Converse by the late 1920s. He sent photos home to his mother, Aurilla, in Columbus. One showed him on the hood of a new Chevrolet, its black enamel coat gleaming in the sun, and additional pictures of himself in a bathing suit show him frolicking near a pool or pier, usually with an attractive young woman in tow. Cars and women would continue to be themes throughout Chuck's life. For example, the second lead story on page 1 of the *Indianapolis Sunday Star* for October 4, 1931 spotlighted a fatal car crash that involved Chuck while he was en route to Bloomington for an Indiana University football game against Notre Dame the day before. Taylor was identified with the Converse Rubber Co. in the text. "Taylor's car was said to have struck the automobile driven by Woolsley squarely on the side, dragging it fifty feet before Taylor's car left the road and overturned several times as it careened over an eight-foot embankment." A passenger in the Woolsley car was killed; a young woman, "Miss Pettibone, 24, of Richmond," was seriously injured while riding in Taylor's car. The lead story for the day was the game score, however—Notre Dame trounced I.U. 25-0.[28]

In time, the names Converse, Chuck Taylor, and All Star were to become inextricably linked. Chuck was to become famous for crisscrossing the country in only the finest automobiles, a suitcase in his back seat and a thick sample case of All Stars competing for space in his trunk alongside a new passion in his life, golf clubs. For years, Converse listed no home address for Chuck, only the downtown Chicago (and later Melrose Park, Illinois) regional headquarters.

"He had a locker in the warehouse and he would exchange clothes depending on the season," recalled Joe Dean, retired athletic director at Louisiana State University, who worked with Taylor at Converse for many years beginning in the early 1950s. "He would live in a hotel 365 days a year. He didn't have a home or apartment until he moved to Port Charlotte, Florida. That's how he lived. He was just a nomad."

That's all largely true, though Chuck was to settle down beginning in 1950, purchasing an upscale home in Los Angeles after his first marriage to bit movie actress Ruth Alder. Later, he went into semi-retirement in Port Charlotte, Florida, with his second wife, Lucy, after the two purchased a four-bedroom ranch home on the first hole of a local golf course community in 1962. But the 1920s were important for Chuck Taylor in that he changed from being an itinerant basketball player to becoming a successful businessman. He traded in his heavy twill basketball trunks and wool jerseys for finely tailored suits, long coats, and Stetson hats. And it was in the 1930s, when Converse and much of the rest of the country struggled through major convulsions because of the Great Depression, that Taylor not only firmly established his new persona, but literally saved the company as well.

The Invisible Pass

The Great Depression spelled doom for some, opportunity for others. For Chuck Taylor, it was the time of his life. Marquis Converse had lost his company in 1928 after it went into receivership. The company's failure was linked to an ill-fated effort to market an automobile tire, the "Converse Cord," which had high production costs, a high failure rate, and many returns from local dealers.

Mitchell B. Kaufman, president and owner of the Hodgman Rubber Co. in Framingham, Massachusetts, bought the firm in 1929, but he sold it to the Stone family—Joseph, Harry K., and Dewey D. Stone—in 1933. The Stone family ran the business for the next thirty-nine years, but in spirit, and in the public's mind, it was to be Chuck Taylor's company from then on.

Chuck's secret was in sales and promotion. Years of touring with the Converse All-Stars basketball squad, making "special appearances" on local hoops teams and glad-handing customers in small-town sporting goods stores, plus his growing number of basketball clinics, were making Chuck a celebrity, albeit a faux celebrity. Converse revamped everything beginning in 1932 to revolve around their new star. The annual Converse Basketball Yearbook, begun in 1922 and enlarged and expanded in 1929, soon began promoting Chuck's clinics, complete with endorsements from top coaches of the day. Beginning in 1932, Chuck's name was added to the ankle patch of the All Star shoe for the first time. His well-regarded College All-American picks began that year as well, next to a smiling mug shot that was to become a signature piece over the years. As if to an increasing drumbeat, Chuck was exclusively touted as a veteran of the great pre–modern era basketball teams, as well as an authority who personally knew the top coaches and best players across the country.

Chuck's clinics, which began informally at North Carolina State in 1922, became more institutionalized in the 1930s. Chuck, or a local sporting goods store, would buy an ad in the paper, or perhaps plant a story with a friendly reporter on a slow news day, and announce that a famous basketball man, one who had allegedly learned his craft with the "world champion" New York Original Celtics or the "Olympic champion" Buffalo Germans, would be in town to offer a free basketball clinic. No admission ever was charged, and the advance publicity always stressed "the fundamentals." The clinics, held in high school and college gyms and often assisted by varsity players, were so non-threatening that for years Chuck didn't even sell shoes at them directly—he just sent prospective customers to the sponsoring local retailer.

Clinics were held from Zanesville, Ohio, to Waco, Texas,

and from Hattiesburg, Mississippi, to San Jose, California. Beginning some time in the 1930s, the clinics started featuring "talking movies," as they were first touted, then simply "filmed highlights" from the previous season's best basketball tournaments. A favorite during the 1950–51 season, for example, were highlights of Nat Holman's City College of New York's dual NIT and NCAA championships the previous year.[1]

Harold "Bunny" Levitt is a former Converse employee who once sank 499 free throws in a row at a YMCA meet in Chicago in 1935, then made a couple of hundred more before calling it a day (requiring seven and a half hours for the entire demonstration). Abe Saperstein, then owner of the Chicago-based Harlem Globetrotters, was so impressed with the feat that he hired Levitt to put on halftime shows for the Globetrotters throughout the mid- and late 1930s. After the war, Levitt went to work for Converse, where he co-hosted clinics with Chuck or did them on his own. Levitt said many of the latter-day clinics were held on school days as part of scheduled assemblies—classes would be cancelled for a period or two and the entire enrollment would pour into the gym or auditorium.

The clinics were marketing tools, for sure, but to Chuck they were like performances. He was Laurence Olivier and Sarah Bernhardt rolled into one; the hardwood court was his stage. Former DePaul University head basketball coach Ray Meyer remembered being called out of the stands while still a college student to assist Chuck during one clinic. "When I was at Notre Dame I was the guy he picked out of the crowd and I couldn't stop his passes," Meyer said. "He was a great ball handler. That was my junior year. It was 1937."

Dwight Hauff, who founded Mid-America Sports in Sioux City, Iowa in 1933 and met Chuck soon thereafter, remembered Taylor's easygoing style, tasteful business attire off-court, and willingness to make appearances in his store as part of a high school or college presentation. "Basically he was not a great athlete," Hauff said. "He was a promoter. His work with Converse in most cases was promotion. He was a good salesman. Anybody that could get Chuck had it made."

Typical garb for hosting a basketball clinic was a knit shirt embroidered with the Converse name and long sweat pants plus, of course, the shoe. "Everything was so quiet when Chuck was on the floor," former Fort Wayne Piston and former Converse executive Bob Houbregs recalled. "All you'd hear is the ball bouncing and shoes squeaking. When Chuck would speak everything would turn quiet." Though Chuck was from Kentuckiana, Bob Houbregs and others recall that his diction was quite neutral, and that his voice was soft, right between a baritone and a tenor. He did not speak loudly, but his voice carried well.

Chuck may have invented the basketball clinic, but he really was following in the footsteps of countless other "demonstrators," from salesmen at county fairs who'd show modern kitchen utensils to rural housewives, to Duncan yo-yo demonstrators who'd put on "contests" at local drugstores and five-and-dimes across the country. A fellow named Ben Pearson was the Chuck Taylor of archery, an ambassador for that sport much as Chuck was an ambassador for basketball. "Ben toured the country and put on trick shot exhibitions while promoting the sport," said Larry Weindruch, a spokesman for the National Sporting Goods Association. "At Ben's posthumous induction, his son talked about some of the trick shots he made look easy, including hitting Ping-Pong balls in mid-air."[2]

Trick shots—that's what Chuck Taylor did too. Pat Harmon first attended a Chuck Taylor clinic while in high school. "Taylor was exciting," he wrote shortly after Chuck's death in

1969. "I've never seen another man do these things: Dropkick a ball into the basket from 50 feet. Bounce a ball into the basket from 70 feet. Throw the ball into the basket from 30 feet while standing with his back to the basket and blindfolded."[3]

Chuck would make backhanded free throws on one bounce from one end of the court to the basket at the other end. He allegedly could pass a ball underneath a car and it would reach the other side before touching the ground. One trick, part of the standard Taylor repertoire for years that Harmon witnessed, was to challenge an entire high school or college team, five on one, to see who could sink the first basket. Chuck would take possession of the ball first, then dribble, fake, and shoot. Harmon witnessed the maneuver successfully employed against the starting University of Cincinnati team one year—Chuck was fifty-one years old at the time.

Another crowd-pleasing joke Chuck would play on an unsuspecting volunteer was to call a boy from the stands, then run to his left, then to his right, and the kid, no matter whether a street urchin or the star player on the host school's team, could not stop him. After embarrassing the boy, Chuck would theatrically walk back toward him, tuck the basketball on one hip and fold his free hand on his other hip, and look straight down at the kid's shoes. "That's what the problem is. He doesn't have Converse All Stars on," he'd declare to the delight of the crowd.

Roy Witry, a four-time letterman in both football and basketball at Anderson High School in Indiana in the late 1930s, recalled that Taylor visited his school every year. The Anderson boys always wore Converse Chuck Taylor All Star shoes, and Chuck once personally chastised Witry when he caught the youngster wearing another company's leather basketball shoes. Chuck noticed things like that. He told young

Witry not to wear them, which Witry said had been a prized gift that were even more pricey than the All Star shoes. "Who am I to turn down an all-leather basketball shoe?" Witry recalled in 2003. "The only problem was they had a felt seam at the bottom of the shoe. If you cut real quick you'd slip." In any case, Witry returned to the All Star posthaste.

A collection of endorsements for the clinics published in the Converse yearbooks of the early 1930s included words from famous coaches such as North Carolina's Gus TeBell, H. C. Carlson of Pittsburgh, H. G. Olsen of Ohio State, and others. Carlson, in particular, marveled at Chuck's "display of passing by peripheral vision, vertically and horizontally."[4]

Indeed, Chuck's passing game always impressed. He made plenty of crowd-pleasing trick shots during his clinics, but the real message was the pass. For example, the script for an undated radio spot that Converse used to promote upcoming clinics claimed it was Taylor who first introduced the one-handed pass to the game.[5] Another source lauded Taylor's "puzzling passes."[6] But the best name of all for Chuck's passing game was "the invisible pass."[7]

That's what a small item in a Kansas newspaper dubbed it in late 1945 when it plugged an upcoming Chuck Taylor clinic. *The invisible pass.* That must be the one Ray Meyer couldn't stop in 1937.

The Converse Basketball Yearbooks, launched in 1922 and lasting all the way to 1983, were a testament to Chuck's growing influence in the 1930s. Whereas the earlier "Reach Guide" (from yet another sporting goods company) emphasized thorough team rosters and year-end summaries for early professional leagues annually until it ceased publication in 1926, Converse's product evolved into a stylish, large-format publication that included hundreds of thumbnail photos of high school and college teams from across the country in each volume, along with brief summaries of the previous season or expectations for the next. Each issue also contained five or six full-length feature articles on game theory and strategy written by the best-known coaches of the day—Converse, and Chuck, just kept spreading the gospel. Though Chuck was never editor (that was Wallace R. Lord for many years), his name and face were all over the publication. Various shoe models (such as the Hickory, Dodger, and Non-Skid, in addition to the All Star) were promoted throughout the yearbook in the early years, before Converse concentrated on pushing the All Star once Chuck's signature was added to the ankle patch. And, from 1932 forward, the front of the book also touted Chuck's college All-American selections. In the initial years Chuck only selected stars he had actually seen play, and he always confirmed his selections with leading coaches of the day. The marketing value of that ploy should be obvious—a coach had to invite him to his school if there was to be any chance for one of his players to be picked, and Chuck could always insinuate himself into any coach's or athletic director's office under the pretext of consulting about an All-American selection.

The All-American lists (along with other lists from the Helms Athletic Foundation and the All-American Board of select big-city sportswriters) were popular in their day. Former Boston Celtics coach Arnold "Red" Auerbach said Chuck's list was particularly important because it was the only one to routinely include stars from the South, Southeast, Far West, and other regions largely overlooked by the New York writers. Former Western Kentucky University star Carlisle Towery remembered when his college told him he had been selected to Chuck Taylor's All-American list in 1941, shortly before he shipped off to war in Europe, where he earned the Bronze Star in battle. "I thought it was about as high an honor as you could get while playing college basketball," he said.

Copies of the Converse Basketball Yearbook now are rare, though tens of thousands were mailed to coaches, players, and fans annually. (Coaches received the first copy free in the early days, and additional samples were 25 cents each.[8]) Converse, Inc., the Naismith Memorial Basketball Hall of Fame, and the University of Notre Dame have the most complete extant collections.

Articles published in the yearbooks always were taken seriously. Arthur L. Trester, secretary of the Indiana High School Athletic Association and a future Hall of Famer himself, wrote about "The Promotion of Basketball in a Public School System" in the 1924 issue, and Marion Crawley, well-known basketball coach at Washington (Ind.) High School, wrote in the 1942 issue about "Methods and Fundamentals That Develop High School Champions," a testament to the regard with which Indiana high school basketball was held generally, as well as a testament to Chuck's loyalty to his Hoosier roots.

In one 1931 tirade, Notre Dame basketball coach George Keogan blasted officiating. Leo Fischer, sports editor of the *Chicago Herald-American,* introduced the "Negro" Washington Bears in the 1943 issue. The Bears had just won the important World Professional Basketball Tournament in Chicago against mostly all-white teams (but also against the better-known all-black Harlem Globetrotters, who at one time were a serious and competitive team). Tennessee A&I coach Johnny McClendon dissected the "two in the corner" offense in the 1957 yearbook. McClendon was promoted not as a black or Negro expert, but as an expert's expert on the game.[9]

John Wooden studied the yearbooks religiously. "You'd

get ideas from other coaches and whatnot," he said. "There weren't a great number of books as you found when years went by. I have about 50 books just from coaches, but at one time I had a stack of Converse yearbooks."

The outstanding feature of the Converse Basketball Yearbook, though, was that a team could get its team picture in it even if it was from an obscure high school or small college. It would be published right alongside the famous college teams of the day and, eventually, top professional teams. You and George Mikan in the same publication, you and Bill Russell in the same publication. There was no cost at all to have a team picture inserted either. There were only two requirements:

"1. Playing data and team pictures must be sent in immediately at close of basketball season.

2. Pictures submitted must show majority of players wearing Converse shoes."[10]

It was more marketing genius from the folks at Converse.

The clinics and yearbooks were effective marketing tools, and the Converse name not only survived, but prospered. Yet Chuck had an additional insight that helped ensure the shoe's success. He explained the guts of the program in his Hall of Fame acceptance speech in 1969. A quality product, attention to detail, and what would be called today good customer service earned Converse lots of sales, but it was an idea that had even escaped Marquis Converse that led to the shoe's greatest success. The retail store owner who ordered the shoe was not the real customer, Chuck concluded, because he wasn't the end user. The kid who actually wore the shoe might be the end user, but he didn't have any money. In a brilliant insight into the demand side of the retail business, Chuck understood it was the high school and college basketball coach who really held sway as to which shoe got worn and which didn't. Chuck recreated a conversation with his beloved mother from early in his sales career.

"Who needs these shoes?" Aurilla had once asked him at the outset of his sales career, Chuck told the Hall of Fame audience.

"Basketball players," Chuck had replied.

"Who buys them for the players?" Mom asked further.

"The coach and high school officials," Chuck answered.

"I think you've been going to the wrong people. Why don't you go to the coaches and show them your shoes?" Mom suggested.[11]

This is just how Chuck and other top salesmen at Converse eventually moved their wares—they went straight to the coaches. Dean Smith, retired Hall of Fame coach at the University of North Carolina, recalled the specific instructions Converse salesmen gave when he ordered shoes as an assistant coach at the Air Force Academy in the mid-1950s. "Bob Davies told us how to write the order so that only Converse could get the sale," Smith recalled. "We even put in that they had to have the Chuck Taylor autograph. But the first year we got lacrosse shoes instead. We didn't get the 'Chucks' until later."

The support of coaches was so important to the brand that when Chuck "upstaged" Kansas basketball coach Forrest "Phog" Allen at a clinic the two men hosted in the early 1950s, Allen retaliated by refusing to order the All Star shoe for his team the following year. This greatly troubled Converse executives because all the high school and small-college coaches in Kansas followed Allen's lead—if he wouldn't order the shoes for his players, neither would they. Three times Chuck apologized. Allen finally ordered the shoes, but only on the condition that Chuck not receive a commission from the sale.[12] Dean Smith, who played for Allen from 1949 to 1953, remembered the episode well, but didn't know all the details for half a century. "We had to switch quickly to Keds," he said. "We didn't get the 'Chucks' back until later."

Yet the company really did make a good product—the double-wall canvas fabric was plenty strong, and old-timers to this day insist the shoes had the best fit of any athletic shoe. "We never got the same fit with the leather shoes that we did with the canvas," recalled Marv Harshman, retired basketball coach at Pacific Lutheran and Washington State Universities, who personally knew Taylor.

But to really make the coaches indebted to Converse, the company simply gave large sums of money to their first national organization, the National Association of Basketball Coaches. The payments reached $50,000 annually. "Converse was the only company that did a lot for the NABC," Harshman said. "Actually, we got about half of our annual budget to run the annual convention. Speaking for myself, we wore Converse because of that. I know when Adidas and Reebok came along I still tried to be loyal to Converse."

The NABC was founded in 1927 by "Phog" Allen, and the organization held its first conference at the Windemere Hotel in Chicago in 1928. In 1939 the group staged its first National Tournament in Evanston, Illinois, but the NCAA soon took over the event—it's the Final Four today.[13] The money Converse gave annually to the NABC was critical for the organization's survival. Ray Meyer recalled that it was Converse executive Grady Lewis who handled the payments in later years. "Grady donated a lot of money to the NABC . . . they made large contributions," Meyer said. "They were very helpful with the basketball coaches when they started organizing basketball."

Other veterans of the game and the industry tell the same story. Bob Steenson, a longtime executive with Converse and unofficial company historian, also confirms that Converse made contributions to the NABC. "If you say Converse sup-

69

ported the NABC, absolutely," Steenson said, but he distinguished between contributions to an organization and later payments other companies made to individual schools and coaches. "When everyone else was accused of paying coaches and paying teams Converse was the last holdout before that thing blew wide open. Converse held out until the very end."

Though Chuck's fame was assured by the 1930s, a surprising controversy was to dog his 1932 signature later in life. Many people consider the Chuck Taylor name to represent the most successful athletic endorsement of all time. Long before Michael Jordan had his line of shoes, there were "Chucks," as they typically were known in many areas, or "Chuck Taylors," as they often were called in inner-city neighborhoods. Golf clubs have long had endorsements, as have tennis racquets, baseball gloves, and bats. But more than 750 million Converse All Star shoes have been sold to date with Chuck's name on them, and there simply is no other example of a largely unchanged model of sports equipment garnering those kinds of numbers. (It is Chuck's signature, too—it matches the handwriting on his 1957 divorce papers and personal letters he wrote later in life.)

The controversy? Did Chuck Taylor receive a royalty for the use of his name? Most knowledgeable sources believe he did not. Gloria Schroeder, the longtime nurse for Chuck's widow, said Lucy Taylor Hennessey often asked Chuck about the royalties during Chuck's lifetime, but he would never discuss the issue. Chuck's stepson, Alan Kimbrell, a St. Louis attorney, also questioned how the most famous shoe endorsement in history could provide for no royalties. "He never really did talk about the royalties," said Kimbrell. "I talked to my mother once about it and she said, 'Well, he just signed something. He never complained about it. He never talked about it. He didn't seem bitter.' I'm a lawyer and the first thing I wonder is, 'Wait a minute. They're selling millions of these shoes with his name on it and he's not getting a dime?' I wondered how good this piece of paper that he signed was."

Chuck almost certainly received royalties in the 1930s, however, after working on commission during the 1920s. He had helped build the brand as no other salesman had, and that is the likely reason he was rewarded in 1932 by having his name put on the shoe. Besides, he had an association with Wilson Sporting Goods Co. in the '30s and ran several sideline businesses from his parents' home in Columbus during that decade. It's only logical that he was working on a royalty basis with Converse. After the war? That was different—that's when Chuck waived his royalty (whatever it had amounted to) in favor of a fixed income of salary, 100 percent expense account, and annual bonuses. As long as Chuck got to talk basketball with sportswriters and coaches across the country, and so long as he was "somebody" when he entered a room filled with sports-minded individuals everywhere, it was enough. The money was secondary.

In any case, internal Converse documents and Chuck's divorce papers show that he grossed between $17,000 and $25,000 per annum throughout the '50s, which is the period when he had clearly abandoned his royalty.[14] A new, fully loaded Lincoln Continental would have cost about $5,000 in those days.

"I don't think anyone in the company coerced [Chuck] to do what he did," said Grady Lewis. "Whatever royalty they paid him, it wasn't great. He decided to take a flat salary and bonuses and expenses."

Converse survived the Great Depression and in fact flourished during World War II as a prime supplier to the military for everything from shearling-lined flying boots and rubberized ponchos to millions of "Chuck Taylors" for GI recreational use (see Appendix for a full company history).

Chuck Taylor prospered in other ways during the 1930s. He was driving nicer cars then, dressing better (solid-color two-piece suits, often light in color, were his preference), and he was even wearing stylish Stetson hats. He took up golf, too—one story recounts how he stopped in French Lick, Indiana while on a business trip from Memphis to Syracuse, paid $5 to enter an amateur golf tournament, and won a watch. When he was invited to return the next day as a finalist he said he couldn't—he had to be in Syracuse the next morning.[15]

His parents had moved to a modern brick Swiss chalet–style home he purchased for them in a solidly middle-class, leafy street a couple of miles north of his old high school in Columbus (coincidentally called Pearl Street, the same street name as for Converse headquarters in Malden, Massachusetts). Chuck ran all his business sidelines out of that home for years—the city directory simply listed the "Chuck Taylor Co." at the same address as for his parents.

Chuck's business interests were many, and he was a one-man growth industry for Columbus. He began marketing his own line of golf clubs for Wilson, and he designed a rounder, firmer basketball for Wilson in 1935.[16] He produced for years a line of wooden golf tees that were shaped from good Indiana hardwood, and Chuck and Carl Hertel co-founded a sheepskin knee pad company in the late '20s that employed more than a dozen women and boys, who cut and sewed the pieces in a Columbus garage. Basketball players often wore knee pads in the early days because it was a rougher game then, and it was not uncommon to slide on the floor in a mad scramble to retrieve a loose ball. "We were the largest makers of those things in the world," Hertel said in a 1987 newspaper interview.[17] The knee pads existed, all right—Francis "Hooley" Gilmore, who had caddied for Chuck in Columbus as a boy, helped make them in the 1930s, and he still had a pristine, unused sample in his possession as late as 2001.[18]

The decade of the 1930s was, in a sense, the glory years for Chuck Taylor. He was at the pinnacle of his fame, and he was eating it up. He had not become the great player he had hoped to be when he left Columbus at age seventeen, but he found recognition in the sport anyway. World War II was on the horizon and it was to change millions of lives forever, including Chuck's. Yet it was just this conflagration that was to provide his greatest challenge on the court, and to prove to the world that Chuck Taylor was not merely a smooth-talking salesman with lots of moxie, but a truly great basketball man in his own right.

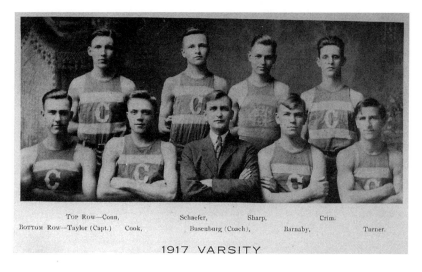

Top Row—Conn,   Schaefer,   Sharp,   Crim.
Bottom Row—Taylor (Capt.)   Cook,   Busenburg (Coach),   Barnaby,   Turner.

1917 VARSITY

Fig. 1. 1917 Columbus High School varsity
basketball team. Taylor is bottom left.

Fig. 2. Chuck Taylor
in Akron, Ohio, ca.
1921. Photo courtesy
Converse, Inc.

Fig. 3. Chuck Taylor "Converse All Stars," 1926–27.

Fig. 4. Snapshot of Chuck Taylor at left, ca. 1917–18 in Columbus, Indiana. The young woman is believed to be younger sister Elsie Taylor, and the young man in the bow tie is believed to be older brother Howard Taylor.

Fig. 5. Chuck Taylor sitting on a Chevy in
Ohio, ca. 1930.

Fig. 6. Chuck Taylor ca. 1930s, woman unknown.

Fig. 7. Lucy Kimbrell (Taylor), seated.

Fig. 8. Wright Field, Dayton, Ohio, ca. 1945. Taylor is in the middle; the man to the left is Dike Eddleman, University of Illinois star. The man Taylor is pointing to is Ed Sadowski, a former Seton Hall star who played for the Detroit Eagles under Coach "Dutch" Dehnert and later for the Boston Celtics. Photo courtesy Diana Eddleman Lenzi.

Fig. 9. Photo of Coach John Wooden autographed to Taylor. "To Chuck Taylor, A friend, fellow-Hoosier, and a kindred soul of basketball. Best wishes always in all ways. Johnny Wooden."

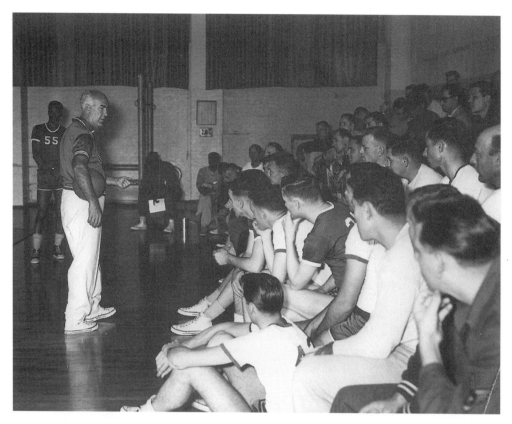

Fig. 10. Taylor leading a basketball clinic ca. late 1950s.

Fig. 13. Chuck and Lucy Taylor at home in Port Charlotte, Florida, ca. 1969. He had just won induction to the Naismith Memorial Basketball Hall of Fame.

OPPOSITE PAGE:

Fig. 11. (TOP) South America tour ca. 1957. Taylor is second from the right; to his left is Felicio Torregrosa, his interpreter from Puerto Rico.

Fig. 12. (BOTTOM) 1969 Hall of Fame induction featuring, from left to right, "Red" Auerbach, "Dutch" Dehnert, "Hank" Iba, Adolph Rupp, and Chuck Taylor.

Special Service

5.

Word of Alabama's clash with the Texas A&M Aggies in the upcoming Cotton Bowl dominated the front sports page of the *Nevada State Journal* on Dec. 2, 1941. But it was an item running down the left side that garnered more attention from a core group of basketball enthusiasts in Reno that day. The brief story hailed a clinic at the University of Nevada gymnasium the night before conducted by Chuck Taylor, America's "ambassador of basketball" and veteran of the best early professional cage teams. A photo showed Chuck in tight-fitting shorts and leather knee pads, plus his own brand of black Converse Chuck Taylor All Star shoes. Forty years old at the time, the 6-foot-1 ex-forward had a deeply receding hairline and was starting to carry a paunch, but he could still rouse interest in the 400 fans who showed up at the Nevada gymnasium, and he could still do free throws from behind his back and dozens of trick passes no youthful defenders could ever seem to stop.[1]

It was to be the last clinic Chuck offered prior to America's entry into World War II. The Japanese attack on Pearl Harbor on December 7, 1941 changed everything. Chuck Taylor's life was changed, too. Past his prime on the "date which will live in infamy," as President Franklin Delano Roosevelt called it, Taylor was too old to fight, yet his patriotism could not be doubted. His older brother, Howard, had been injured in France during World War I while Chuck was still shooting hoops for the Bull Dogs of Columbus High School. Now it was Chuck's turn to serve.

In time the government would provide an important avenue for aging professional athletes and well-known coaches to assist in the war effort via the Special Services Division of the Army Service Forces. Chuck Taylor was about to put on a very different uniform than the ones he had worn on the Akron Firestone Non-Skids or Converse All-Stars in the 1920s.

Special Services was established in 1942 on the recommendation of the Joint Army and Navy Committee (the JANC) on Welfare and Recreation, which itself had been established shortly before World War II in anticipation of the looming conflict. From the early days of the war, Special Services was charged with developing a program to keep soldiers busy, happy, and fit when they were not fighting, and it even had its own training school at Fort Meade, Maryland.[2] "Every red-blooded American youth, in and out of uniform, is a lover of sports," a Special Services booklet published during the war declared. "The Army has found it desirable to maintain and foster this competitive ideal. Mass participation in sports and games of every description is the Army goal."[3]

Eleven million Americans suited up during World War II, and most of them, in one way or another, were touched by Special Services, which operated at virtually every camp, base, fort, and command post at home and abroad, and even assigned officers full-time to manage its affairs at the various military installations. Self-contained Special Services companies traveled through operational theaters abroad with athletic equipment, as well as books, records, and even 16mm films. From February 1942 to April 1944, $20 million worth of athletic supplies were shipped out by the Kansas City quartermaster, including $1 million worth of softballs and $1.7 million in basketballs and footballs.[4] Fifty two fieldhouses for camps with more than 10,000 men were ordered built early in the war.[5] Thousands of pairs of basketball shoes were shipped to military bases from Miami to San Diego; even American troops caught in North Africa during the middle of the war clamored for shipments of basketballs from Special Services. Hoops were such a huge hit among the soldiers during the winter of 1942–43, the first full winter for America at war, that the Special Services Division ordered an "Official Basketball Guide for 1943–44," which would standardize rules for all base competition and service leagues. This may have been the first truly standardized rules book in the history of the game (college, pro, and even different leagues previously had their own rules), and it may have helped set the stage for the emerging popularity of professional basketball after the war.[6]

Donald W. Rominger, Jr., a young doctoral student at Oklahoma State University in 1976, studied the War Department's commitment to sport during World War II and concluded it was all about one thing—victory under arms. Special Services simply took the YMCA and "college man" model of sport as activities that built good character and developed strong leadership skills and raised it to the next level. "Athletic events, representing the spirit of the American past, were used to train troops, raise war funds, satisfy public morale and physically equip the young generation . . . ," Rominger wrote. "Sport was believed to have unique qualities representing the moral and physical superiority of the United States. Therefore the nation's institutional leaders and its government worked to unleash and develop sport and physical training around the war effort."[7]

Most of the competition was at the level of intramurals, as they would be called on college campuses today, but every command post had its majordomo teams, which rivaled the service academies and major colleges for attention during the war and attracted big crowds to their games. "Tony" Hinkle instructed the best players at the Great Lakes Naval Training Station north of Chicago, winning the national armed services championship during the 1942–43 season.[8] Everett Case coached at DePauw Naval Training Station and Ottumwa (Iowa) Naval Air Station during World War II—he won the armed services championship in the 1945–46 season.[9] Contemporaneously with these two men was a friend common to both, also from Indiana—shoe salesman Charles H. "Chuck" Taylor. He was tapped by Army Air Force Commanding General H. H. "Hap" Arnold to coach the Air-Tecs of Wright Field in Dayton, Ohio, which was the top Air Force command post team during the war. For one glorious season during 1944–45, after serving as a recruiter and physical fitness expert for two years for the Navy, Chuck toured with a stable of some of the best All-American basketball players in the country, several of whom he had known before the war, as far south as Florida and Texas and as far west as California. The Air-Tecs, so-named for the Air Technical

Service Command in Dayton, was not only to prove itself the best service team in history—better than Hinkle's nationally known Great Lakes Bluejackets—but one of the best teams in the history of collegiate or professional basketball ever. Yet the team was forgotten—completely forgotten—for decades. For all the nonsense about Chuck Taylor's alleged role with the Original Celtics and the Buffalo Germans, and all the questions surrounding his surprise selection to the Naismith Memorial Basketball Hall of Fame in 1969, Chuck could have shaped his legacy and won his place in history solely on the basis of that single season with the Air-Tecs.

That men like Hinkle, Case, and Taylor would coach service teams, or that strapping young soldiers would be assigned to play on the teams instead of sent in harm's away, may seem surprising, or perhaps a form of self-indulgence by the military. But the War Department actively encouraged the selection of nationally recognized coaches and athletes for command and post teams. A Special Services Division proposal written during the war urged local commanders to "make available" to the program soldiers with experience as players, coaches, or athletic directors.[10]

Coach Hinkle wrote a newspaper article about the basketball programs that was nationally syndicated in 1943. The wide distribution of the article suggests that he, and the Bluejackets, were well known.

"The home front is as important to victory in this war as the battle front. And sports, by its very nature, is a leader in upholding public morale in wartime," wrote Hinkle. "Of all sports played in America basketball is the finest to sustain morale. . . . Basketball is a truly community sport, and because of that fact, will be relied on by a community even more now that gasoline and tires are rationed. Each community in the country will have to furnish its own recreation in a large measure, and basketball is made to order for these wartime conditions.

"The same thing is true in the service. Here at the naval training station at Great Lakes, we consider sports the backbone of our naval community. From the thousands of boys in training, we have drawn more than 1,000 basketball teams."[11]

Special Services also organized boxing matches, as well as football, baseball, and even soccer games, plus arts and crafts classes and music ensembles. But basketball had huge appeal because it was cheap, could be played indoors and out, and did not require complex instruction at the intramural level to master the basics.

The Army programs were so popular, and reached so many Americans, that professional businessmen clamored for a piece of the action. A representative of Charles C. Spink & Son, publishers of *The Sporting News,* wrote Frederick Osborn, head of JANC, requesting membership on the welfare and recreation committee, but he was denied. Top advisory and administrative posts typically were limited to important college administrators and career Army and Navy officers, and occasionally to well-known professional athletes, such as former world professional boxing champion Gene Tunney, who had served as a Marine in World War I. It probably didn't help *The Sporting News* that the writer misspelled Osborn's last name—he placed an "e" at the end of the name in the original letter.[12]

Then there were the promoters who offered to organize their own exhibition games on military bases, typically with free admission for servicemen and women, but not necessarily for the general public that might also attend. John L. Dedeick of Bronx, New York, wrote the director of the Special

Special Service

Services Division in 1944, offering "free exhibition games at Army camps throughout the country." Dedeick claimed to represent top professional basketball teams, including the All-American Red Head Girls, Renaissance Worlds Colored Champions, Philadelphia Hebrews, and Original Celtics. "Our purpose is to offer service men sports recreation in a manner similar to the entertainment provided by USO-Camp shows. Besides building morale, our plan would further the Army's own policy of developing soldier-interest and participation in sports."[13] The proposal was not far-fetched—professional boxer Joe Louis, who often staged exhibition matches on military bases, was booked by the Special Services Division for his appearances months in advance. Dedeick was turned down, though, denying him the right to say he promoted events for the War Department, which in its own way would have been as good then as saying "as seen on TV" is for marketing and self-promotion purposes today.

Chuck Taylor's assignment to Wright Field in December 1944 was his final one during the war. Military personnel records show his dates of service from January 22, 1943 to August 10, 1945. Commissioned as a naval reserve lieutenant initially, he served first with the Naval Aviation Cadet Service Board in Chicago, then at the Naval Air Station in Quonset Point, Rhode Island. He also was with a Civil Aeronautics Authority–War Training Service "V-5" program at Marquette University in Milwaukee, then was a naval cadet pilot recruiter again based in Chicago (working with Everett Case in the same capacity for a time), and finally basketball coach at Wright Field in Dayton, Ohio.[14]

Basically, what Chuck did prior to coaching the Air-Tecs was lead physical fitness classes and recruit Navy pilots. Many celebrities, whether in the entertainment industry or the world of sports, helped recruit during the war. It was an effective tool. For example, a wartime article in Columbus, Indiana touts an Indianapolis appearance by Chuck. It was big news that Chuck Taylor would personally sign you up. "Local young men interested in training as a Navy pilot now have an opportunity to appear before a well-known Columbus man and basketball authority for interviews. The Ninth Naval district headquarters, Cincinnati, Ohio, announced today that Lt. C. H. 'Chuck' Taylor of Columbus will be one of two officers who will interview young men from this area for Navy officer pilot training on Monday and Tuesday of each week. . . . Lt. Taylor, widely-known in basketball circles, gained his reputation after playing on the Columbus high school net team and later as a star with the New York Celtics."[15]

Chuck's duties with would-be pilots at Marquette almost certainly involved coaching basketball as well as running the usual calisthenics and physical fitness programs. Basketball in particular was seen as a useful tool for teaching quick reflexes and good eye-hand coordination to pilots during the war.[16] The "V" programs had their origins in 1939, when Congress authorized the Civil Aeronautics Administration (sometimes called Civil Aeronautics Authority) to create a civilian pilots' training course; the V-5 programs also were known as Navy Aeronautics Preflight Schools. There was no aerial training in these "pre-flight" programs, however, only classroom instruction and lots of physical fitness training and sports competitions. About 80,000 cadets and 2,500 instructors worked with V-5 programs across the country, though this is yet another nearly forgotten chapter from World War II.[17] Trainees at Marquette received twelve weeks of ground instruction, then shipped off to a real flight school; there were no airplanes on campus. All told, 747 men trained in the V-5 program at Marquette from 1942 to 1945.[18]

Most recreational and physical fitness programs used high school and college coaches who were conscripted or who joined up during the war. Though he was not a college or high school coach himself, which was almost a union card required for admission to frontlines of Special Services, and even though he was a businessman, who were generally shunned, Chuck had put on all those beloved basketball clinics through the years, and virtually every high school and college hoopster in the nation played in his shoes. Whether Chuck exploited his military service for increased sales or visibility during the war itself is unclear—the Converse Basketball Yearbooks do show him in military garb—yet there's no evidence he lived on his service record after the war. In fact, few sources, including the Hall of Fame in Springfield or the current generation of Converse executives in North Andover, Massachusetts, have any specific information on what he did while in uniform.

The idea of linking sports to war was not new. Gen. John J. Pershing, commander of the American expeditionary forces in Europe during World War I, signed the first General Order (No. 241) relating to sports in the U.S. Army on December 29, 1918, and he supported doughboy participation in track and field events, baseball, basketball, tennis, boxing, and wrestling in the Inter-Allied Games in Paris in June and July 1919. Pershing later authorized what appears to be the first formal agreement between the Army and YMCA for the clear purpose of improving the quality of soldiering.[19]

Many observers spoke of "the fighting spirit," or the need for discipline, or touted other virtues that organized sport and competition would inculcate in the men. Ex-boxer Tunney, a lieutenant commander in the Navy and officer in charge of athletics in the Bureau of Navigation early in World War II, went further than most. He advocated punishing workouts and tireless exercise routines over team play. He made many comments during the war urging government policymakers to toughen up the men, not entertain them. "People of the United States from all walks of life [have] permitted themselves to go soft," Tunney told a government panel in 1941. He urged a program "principally to develop stamina and fighting ability in men."[20]

Yet a darker view also held sway in some quarters, including in General Osborn himself, according to some critics. Osborn headed the JANC throughout the war and encouraged Army chief of staff George C. Marshall to establish a morale branch in the Army and Army Air Force (the branch that became Special Services). A social scientist by training, Osborn had surveyed attitudes among enlisted men and conscripts in the early part of the war and found that many of the soldiers did not, in fact, want to defend democracy, did not like the British or French, whom they were saving, and thought they could be more productive back home in their civilian jobs. The need for "morale" as well as physical fitness training was clear.

Osborn also was a past president of the American Eugenics Society and consequently held controversial views about inherent superiority and inferiority. In brief, eugenics was the belief that people were failures in life because they were genetically deficient, and that the best way to stop undesirable traits from infiltrating society was to keep inferior people from breeding. Osborn was considered a "reform eugenicist," however, because he believed one should nevertheless help inferior people by appropriate training and social engineering. In keeping with this school of thought, Osborn may simply have believed sport and competition would make the average enlisted man a better worker bee or a better second-class citizen. He once wrote that sport and competition were important because "without an adequate substitute for military training, administered with vigor and conviction, cases of absence without leave, desertion, insubordination, petty misdemeanors, and even serious crime" would escalate as had been the case during and immediately after World War I, when General Pershing first identified the need for sport in the American military.[21]

6.

Air-Tecs

Chuck Taylor was sitting on a narrow bench in the cavernous, tile-lined fieldhouse at Wright Field, Ohio in early December 1944, watching his "boys" go through an early evening workout and jawing with a local newspaper reporter. John Mahnken, who not long before was the 6-foot-8 starting center on the Georgetown University Hoyas, "dripped sweat" as Taylor continued sitting on the bench in his birch-colored sweat pants and shirt and egged on Mahnken and the other young basketball stars.

"Lt. Charles (Chuck) Taylor cast a quick glance at Mahnken," the reporter wrote, "and the rest of the basketball players who were rounding out the first scheduled practice of the Air-Tecs, the quintet which will represent the Air Technical Service Command this year against professional, collegiate, and service teams. 'They're getting tired,' he grinned. A minute later he called his team together. 'That's enough for today. You can shoot baskets for a while if you want, but we'll meet here tomorrow same time. Okay? See you tomorrow night.'

"The coach of the newly-organized Air-Tecs paused as some of the players left for showers, others practiced foul shots. 'This'll get them all into condition. Most of the boys are in pretty good shape anyway, but all this running will fix them up.'"[1]

Taylor had been in this mid-Ohio city before, when he made a "special appearance" on the Dayton Kellys semi-pro basketball team, and probably numerous other times on sales calls or to host clinics. Now he was stationed in Dayton, at what was arguably the largest air force base in the world, a vast proving ground for global aerial warfare.

But Chuck was not in Dayton to make war. He had literally been "loaned" by the Navy, according to one newspaper account, to whip up a new Army Air Force service team into such a competitive state that it would take away the glory from the Great Lakes Naval Training Station Bluejackets, then the most popular and widely acclaimed service team (as distinct from military academy) in the country. Chuck's arrival in town was signaled by every Dayton newspaper of the day, which called him a "pioneer" of the sport and more.[2]

What a team it was, bold and prominent in its "AAF blue and yellow" colors. Technical Sergeant Johnny Schick was on it. Schick starred on the Ohio State University team that went all the way to what is now identified as the first NCAA finals in Evanston, Illinois in 1939. (The Buckeyes lost in the championship game to Oregon 46-33.[3])

John Mahnken, the Georgetown center, was to play pro ball after the war, including for the Rochester Royals and Boston Celtics. Ed Sadowski was a former Seton Hall University cager and Detroit Eagles pro star who also later played for the Celtics; at twenty-nine he was the old man on the team. Dwight "Dike" Eddleman, a University of Illinois recruit who dropped out of college at age seventeen to enlist in the Army, joined the Air-Tecs a little later in the season and also was destined to play pro ball later in his career.

Bruce Hale became an Air-Tec in mid-February 1945 after Chuck saw him play with a different service team against the Air-Tecs in Miami. Hale went on to coach in the American Basketball Association (1967–68 Oakland Oaks), but is best remembered as a longtime University of Miami basketball coach. Also playing for the Air-Tecs were George Light, Al Negratti (later with the Rochester Royals), Ralph McNeil, and Roy Witry, the same Roy Witry whom Chuck had personally admonished during a visit to Anderson High School in Indiana for not wearing his Converse Chuck Taylor All Stars.

Chuck had done it again. He had assembled a high-caliber team, a competitive team of the first order. It must have been the most fun he had experienced since touring as player-manager with the Converse All-Stars during the 1926–27 season. But this team was so much better. Plus, he finally would get to show off his basketball knowledge and expertise before a national audience as the Air-Tecs were to play more than fifty games and travel throughout the country that season.

Surviving coaches such as Red Auerbach and John Wooden who personally knew Chuck dispute that he was an important strategist or theorist who improved the game, but you couldn't tell that to Chuck. In particular, Chuck hated "basketball systems." This is remarkable because at every clinic, in every newspaper interview, and in his pocket-sized "Basketball Fundamentals" handbook, he always took pains to stress that his advice was compatible with all "systems," and that he meant neither favoritism nor disparagement toward any.

"He didn't like any system that was so restrictive a player had to take three steps, then pass before he could shoot," recalled former Georgetown College and Auburn University coach Bob Davis. "He said systems were just to keep your players organized. They had to cover the ball and make a fast break. Any time you had a system it should be limited to those things, defensive balance so that you always had somebody back, and offensive rebounding. He liked two people back to stop a fast break, and three people to get an offensive rebound."

Chuck had published "how-to" articles on the game in newspapers across the country beginning in the 1930s.[4] He stressed good passing, looking for the easy layup, and solid physical conditioning, and he could be outspoken in newspaper interviews.

"First they took away the half court from the offensive team by forcing it to move the ball over the center line within 10 seconds," he railed in a 1937 interview. "Then they took still more playing surface away by forbidding a member of the offensive line to stand in his own free throw lane or circle for more than three seconds. I don't know what will be taken away next. . . . The biggest trouble with the game today? Well, I'd say over-officiating. Some of the officials have the idea that the folks paid to hear them blow the whistle."[5]

Talk is cheap, as the saying goes, but now Chuck would have a chance to prove himself. Not just as a great businessman or icon, but as a truly great basketball man. Today Chuck's Air-Tecs would look like a fantasy basketball league team—that's how good they were, that's how improbable was their composition. To top matters off, the Air-Tecs, and Chuck, were to pull off what can only be considered one of the greatest coups (if not outright scams) in the history of organized basketball anywhere, at any time, before the season was over.

Wright Field, now part of Wright-Patterson Air Force Base, was established on the Huffman Prairie near Dayton, exactly where the Wright Brothers built several Wright Flyers in 1904 and 1905 after returning from their successful first powered flight in Kitty Hawk, North Carolina in 1903. Base histories note that during the war Wright Field was a sprawling complex in and of itself, with up to 300 buildings and approximately 45,000 civilian employees and military personnel working on base and at nearby Patterson Field at any one time. The Army Air Corps (later Army Air Force) glommed on to Wright Field as its main proving ground for new aircraft because of its long grass runways; these were, however, quickly paved during the war. A housing shortage, bad everywhere during the conflict and in the years immediately thereafter, was particularly bad in Dayton, a mid-sized industrial city in west central Ohio, but Chuck solved that problem easily—he lived on base, in the senior officers' area.[6]

Wright Field was a command post, perhaps the most important Air Force base in North America. The reason the Air Technical Service Command got Chuck as a coach, and a bench filled with All-Americans and future pros, was the always ambitious, publicity-conscious Army Air Force commander, General H. H. "Hap" Arnold. "By that fall [1944] the Air Branch was committed to the concentration of famous athletes at particular bases, the organization of elite coaching staffs, and the use of transport aircraft to fly teams long distances for play," wrote historian Donald Rominger.[7]

Eddleman, the Illinois teenager who joined the team on a swing through the upper Midwest and Great Plains states, is worth revisiting briefly. His biography, published in 1997, documents the man's brilliant, multi-sport achievements in basketball, football, and track and field, and makes rare historical references to Taylor and the Air-Tecs. The biography, written by Eddleman's daughter, recalls the story of how Dike and Chuck met, though it contains several curious errors of fact.

"While at Scott Field [near Miami], Dike was recruited by Chuck Taylor, former star of the original New York Celtics. Eddleman soon transferred to Wright-Patterson Field in Dayton, Ohio, where he continued his basketball career for the Air Tec Kittyhawk Flyers, one of the nation's greatest service quintets. Taylor, a commissioned Colonel in the Army and a lieutenant in the Navy whose later claim to fame was his affiliation with Converse tennis shoes, coached the Flyers. Taylor said, 'Eddleman is a greater basketball player right now than Hank Luisetti, the famous Stanford player. Give him three more years at the University of Illinois and he'll make you forget the names of a lot of other guys who have played basketball in this country.'"[8]

The *Dayton Daily News, Dayton Herald,* and *Dayton Journal,* plus a Wright Field post newsletter, all followed the team's progress throughout the season. Most contests were against other military teams and college squads.[9] By mid-January 1945 the Air-Tecs (usually spelled with a hyphen, but not always) had an average height of 6 feet 6 inches after adding Chris Hansen ("the Great Dane," formerly of Bradley Tech), and their won-lost record was 15-2.[10]

Roy Witry was added in February. As of 2003 Witry, retired and living in Dallas, Texas, appeared to be the sole surviving Air-Tec. He confirmed Chuck's eye for talent and the Army Air Force's willingness to bend the rules to help Chuck build his team. "I was recruited," said Witry. "I had been down in Texas in evac military aircraft and Tinker Field in Oklahoma. In the beginning they had me in the physical ed department. I played basketball down at Kelly Field. We won everything there was down there. Chris Hansen, who I had been with down in Texas . . . told somebody about me. They cut orders for me, I don't know who, and before I knew it I was at Wright Field."

That somebody had to be Taylor, who clearly was building his team throughout the season. As the "ambassador of basketball," he had traveled the country observing the best high school and college programs, and he had a good memory. Plus, as Eddleman said in his biography, published four years before his death, Taylor had recruited *him*.

The Air-Tecs traveled on well-maintained Air Force transports and stayed at quality hotels, but they were never paid a dime extra for being athletes. As representatives of the U.S. government and all other men and women still in uniform and still in harm's way, they were compelled to be on their best behavior. Eddleman, who was more country than Chuck, would chew tobacco and curse heavily and had to be repeatedly warned to clean up his act in public. Things got silly at times, though, such as at a USO benefit in California that was sponsored by Hollywood actor and showman Joe E. Brown; actress Lucille Ball also was at the event. "A twenty-five-dollar bond would get you the cheapest seat," recalled Witry. The Air-Tecs did not travel with a trainer, but Chuck always tried to recruit one locally. When he couldn't, he filled that role himself, even personally rubbing down the feet of his players, Witry said. Before this particular game, Chris Hansen was getting a rubdown on a table in the locker room. He was naked, and Lucille Ball came to the door. "Coach said, 'You can't come in,'" recalled Witry. "'We've got men with no clothes on.' She said, 'I don't care. I've seen it all already,' and she burst right in. So coach said, 'Well, I guess you have seen it all.'"

The Air-Tecs played their home games at the Montgomery County Fairgrounds Coliseum, which seated about 3,000 fans. It was the same venue Chuck had played in during the Kellys game in December 1927, and it also was home to Dayton's independent professional basketball team, the Acme Aviators. (That was their real name; the Aviators were sponsored by the Acme Aluminum Co.) Sometimes, the two teams clashed. In their first matchup in February 1945, Chuck's Air-Tecs easily bested the professionals, who only the previous year had competed in the highly regarded World Professional Basketball Tournament in Chicago, falling in the second round to eventual winner Fort Wayne. A reporter covering the game confirmed that the Air-Tecs were "one of the nation's service powerhouse teams," and heaped praise on individual team members. Dike Eddleman was called "an amazing shot." Mahnken was "remarkably well-coordinated." Ed Sadowski, "except for his displays of temperament," was termed the best man in the pivot "since Dutch Dehnert was in his prime." Only Acme player-coach Bob Colburn and center "Wee" Willie Smith were credited with strong showings for the pros.[11]

Serious students of basketball will be surprised to learn that Smith starred in Dayton. This is the same "Wee" Willie Smith who played with the New York Renaissance in the 1930s, starting at center and helping the Rens, as they were commonly known, win eighty-eight games in a row beginning in 1932. He later played alongside William "Pop" Gates, who was elected to the Hall of Fame in 1989. In fact, the Rens were inducted into the Hall of Fame as a team in 1963, and it was they who had won the World Professional Basketball Tournament in Chicago in its inaugural year in 1939. The nickname "Wee" was ironic—Smith was a 6-foot-8, hulking black man with a gentle nature who later was to lose a son during the Vietnam War.

The Air-Tecs were the big buzz in Dayton throughout the winter and early spring of 1945. Their game summaries moved from below the fold to lead stories with headlines stripped across the top of the *Dayton Daily News* sports section. "Dayton fans now realize why the Air-Tecs, under the coaching of Lt. Chuck Taylor, have been rolling over all kinds of opposition from coast to coast and recently received an invitation to an all-service tournament in Chicago," another important wartime event, one story declared.[12] The invitation actually was expected—that was the tournament Tony Hinkle and his Navy Bluejackets had won before, and that was the title General Arnold wanted in his trophy case. It was why Chuck Taylor was brought to Dayton in the first place.

Chuck was receiving attention off the court in Dayton, too. Tassie Dempsey and her husband, Jimmie, a young B-17 pilot, visited their friend Chuck in 1945. Chuck, who wintered in Florida so he could play golf, owned a twelve-unit apartment building in Sarasota, Florida, and had rented a unit to the Dempseys in 1942, cutting the rent in exchange for Jimmie's gasoline ration card. By 1945 Jimmie was a seasoned pilot who had been temporarily assigned to Wright Field, and he and his wife visited with Taylor. The always gracious basketball coach treated them to dinner at a local hotel.

"He was a low-key, sweet, gentle somebody," Tassie recalled. "I never saw him lose his temper save for one time. It was in Dayton. The man was very unruly and rude. Chuck said, 'If you say one more word I'm going to pick you up and throw you in that seat.' We all were just so shocked. He never raised his voice."

The Air-Tecs continued their winning ways—they won fifty-five games all told during the season, according to one source.[13] The team won a laugher in San Bernardino, California against the 21st Ferrying Group in a fund-raiser for wounded soldiers on February 24, and Taylor put all the players he had with him on the court at one point or another during the game—including himself. In what may be the last competitive basketball game Chuck Taylor ever played, he scored a single basket during this contest. He was forty-three years old at the time. The box score doesn't identify which position he played or how many minutes he had—for decades basketball box scores failed to identify minutes played.[14]

The Air-Tecs must have been looking forward to the all-service invitational tournament to be held in Chicago that spring. They were selected for the competition along with the Bluejackets, of course, as well as several other important service squads.[15] Service teams were closely watched by the basketball public during the war, and the Converse Basketball Yearbook ranked top service teams just as they ranked top college teams. But the Air-Tecs couldn't go to the all-service team invitational after all. The Air Force grounded them and all other Army Air Force basketball teams on March 1, 1945.

"Headquarters in Washington ordered all air force basketball teams to quit playing away from their home installations as of March 1. It is believed, however, that such teams may still play in their home cities, so the Tecs are likely to be seen in a game or two, locally."[16]

The Air-Tecs could not disobey orders. There was a war going on. They only were allowed to travel around the country playing other teams because the War Department wanted to boost morale, and the games were important fund-raisers for unbudgeted items in the military. Nevertheless, temperamental ex-pro ballplayer Ed Sadowski had an idea. He had furlough coming up. He had a friend, Buddy Jeannette, currently on the Fort Wayne Pistons, the defending champions of the World Professional Basketball Tournament. Jeannette and Sadowski had been teammates on the Detroit Eagles, where the two men had helped that team win the tournament in 1941.[17] Sadowski decided to take his leave in March and quietly travel to Chicago to play with his old friend on the Pistons. Sadowski may have been driven by pique at the Air Force or perhaps loyalty to his old friend Jeannette. Or it may have been the prize money if the Pistons won again. The 1945 tournament victors were guaranteed $2,000, real money in those days, and even the runner-ups garnered $1,500.[18]

Chuck Taylor knew about the pro tourney, held every March in Chicago, and not for the obvious reason that all pro basketball fans of the era followed it. He had a more intimate connection. Tournament promoters Harry Hannin and Leo Fischer, along with the de facto publicist for the tourney, *Herald-American* sportswriter Jimmy Enright, all contributed articles to the Converse Basketball Yearbook during the war years. It was Enright who had written about future Hall of Famer George Mikan in the 1945 edition. Hannin wrote in the same edition about the "shocking loss" for the College All-Star team the previous December (1944) against the Pistons in an annual charity event also sponsored by the *Herald-American.* Fischer's contribution in the 1943 book was the full-page story about the then current tourney champions, the Washington Bears, one of the all-black basketball teams that competed on an "equal footing" with the white teams in Chicago.

Though grounded, the Air-Tecs still met competition at home, including under unusual circumstances. While most of the soldier-athletes were sitting in the stands at the Fairgrounds Coliseum the first Sunday afternoon in March to watch an Aviators contest against the Cleveland Buckeyes, just like 1,000 or so other spectators that day, they received a verbal request from the referee to come down to the court. It was game time and the Buckeyes were stuck in traffic. Would the available Air-Tec players substitute for the Clevelanders?

"Just returned from an extensive charity tour of the Pacific coast [in late February], the Air Tecs found no peace when they returned to Dayton yesterday," wrote one newspaper reporter. "Acme was scheduled to play the Buckeyes. But with the arrival of game time and not of the Cleveland team a problem presented itself. The fans solved it by getting up a clamoring for the Air Tecs . . . who were in the stands. Coach Bob Colburn of Acme persuaded the soldier-basketeers to send for their equipment to satisfy the Aviators' desire for revenge, the fans' demands and their own cage appetites. They did."[19]

The Air-Tecs spanked the Aviators once again, this time 43-39 (though one paper reported the score as 45-39), and most of the Air-Tec regulars saw action, including Hale, Eddleman, Hansen, Mahnken, and Schick (notably absent was Sadowski). The Buckeyes actually arrived at the venue shortly before the first half ended. There were plenty of seats in the stands and they just sat and watched the game play out.[20]

While it looked like most of the Air-Tecs would be confined to Dayton that spring, the Aviators were preparing for another invitation to the World Professional Basketball Tournament. Robert Colburn, coach Bobby Colburn's son, said his dad signed players by offering them good-paying jobs at the Acme Aluminum factory. "He always told me how good the Aviators were," said Robert Colburn, who still lives in Dayton. "I used to watch all the games at the Coliseum. I was a little young. I spent most of the time playing under the bleachers."

The Aviators had competed in the world tourney the year before, defeating the Akron Collegians 52-38 in the first round before bowing to the Pistons in the quarterfinal round 59-34.[21] Would the Aviators be any more competitive when they got to Chicago this year? After all, they couldn't beat the local service team in two tries. Maybe there was a way. Little clues to the team's strategy began emerging on the pages of the *Dayton Daily News* later in March, as the Aviators prepared for a game against the all-black Chicago Crusaders. "It was Bobby's hope to use the same lineup in this game as he plans to floor in the coming tournament at Chicago the middle of this month and *that would include a number of the Air-Tec cagers.* Some of the Air-Tecs may be available for the Sunday game but the fact still isn't known for sure" (emphasis added).[22]

The game against the Crusaders was a tune-up for the upcoming pro tournament in Chicago, and something was brewing, all right. A later story about the Crusaders game was more blunt, and it revealed conclusively the guiding hand of Chuck Taylor behind a plot to send almost all the Air-Tecs, GIs who were still in military uniform, to compete disguised as the Dayton Acme Aviators in the most famous pro tournament of the era. In the old days this was called "padding" a team.

"As for using several of the Air-Tecs against the Crusaders, Bobbie [*sic*] remarked that 'Taylor (Lt. Chuck Taylor, Tec coach) thought it wouldn't be advisable to put the idea into shape yet. But we'll use them in the pro tourney in Chicago.'"[23]

The contest against the Crusaders soon was followed by a more important event. Three teams bound for the upcoming Chicago pro tourney, the Harlem Globetrotters, the Long Island (N.Y.) Grumman Hellcats, and the Indianapolis Oilers, stopped over in Dayton and put on a double bill with the Aviators at the Coliseum. All these teams were scheduled to appear in Chicago later in the month. In fact, the Aviators were to square off against the Hellcats in the first round at Chicago Stadium.

But it wasn't really the Aviators who showed up at the Montgomery County Fairgrounds Coliseum this time. "The new Acme team is made up of players, for the most part, who starred during the season for the Wright Field Air-Tecs on its swing through the country," announced the *Dayton Daily*

News. "This is the same team that will go on to Chicago for the locals, all the athletes having been *granted furloughs.* Coach Bob Colburn's starting Acme Quintet will include George Light and Hale at the forwards, Long John Mahnken at center, with Al Negratti and Chris Hansen at the guards. Reserve members are Roy Witry, who won't make the trip to the Windy City; Rex Gardecki, a regular Aviator; Johnny Schick and Colburn. . . . [They] should help the local team's chances immeasurably in the tourney" (emphasis added).[24]

Curiously absent from the Aviators lineup was "Wee" Willie Smith, their star center. So where was "Wee" Willie on this day in Dayton? One newspaper item suggested that he was contemplating jumping to the Cleveland Buckeyes team, but that would not have been a smart move—the Buckeyes were not invited to Chicago. In fact, Smith went to Chicago with his old team, the New York Rens, while his old teammate from the Rens, "Pop" Gates, joined the Long Island Grumman Hellcats for the tournament![25]

Witry later explained why he (and Eddleman) chose not to compete in the pro tournament. They didn't want to risk losing their amateur status and NCAA eligibility. Eddleman traveled with the new Aviators to Chicago anyway, but competed instead in a collegiate track and field meet held in the city at the same time.

The newly reconstituted Acme Aviators won their match with the Grumman squad, though it was close, 44-42. And *all* the players who show up on the box score were Air-Tecs; Gardecki and player-coach Colburn never got in the game.[26] Chuck Taylor, and the United States Army Air Force, had simply taken over the team. Their new mission? Conquer the world, not merely other service teams.

7. World Tourney

Pete Ankney was dumbstruck when he saw the Chicago Stadium, that holy shrine to political conventions, college commencement exercises, and basketball games for generations of Chicagoans, for the first time. Located just two miles from downtown on West Madison Street, the stadium was a short taxi ride from the dark, imposing Morrison Hotel in the central business district, where Ankney and the new Acme Aviators from Dayton, Ohio stayed that March in 1945. Ankney, just thirteen at the time, had obtained the job as the Aviators' ballboy through connections—his older sister was married to the team's player-coach, Bobby Colburn—and he had caught a ride to Chicago with his brother-in-law in his maroon-colored Pontiac. Bruce Hale, Johnny Schick, and several other Tecs, as well as Rex Gardecki of the real Aviators, followed along as part of a motor caravan that traveled west on U.S. 40, then took a right turn at U.S. 41 in Terre Haute and went all the way up to Chicago. It would have been a seven-hour trip in those days, on those roads.

Ankney was smitten with Chicago—the tall buildings, the lakefront, and the water shows at Buckingham Fountain in Grant Park, as well as the constant clang and din from the busy commuter trains that ringed the Loop. "I can remember going out by myself in Chicago and buying fried shrimp," said Ankney, who retired as head football coach at the University of Dayton. "It was the first time I ever had shrimp." But most of all, Ankney loved the attention—everybody stared at the basketball players when they got out of a taxi, and people would ask if they were in town for the well-publicized tourney.

The World Professional Basketball Tournament, sometimes called the World Tournament of Professional Basketball, was held annually from 1939 to 1948 in either the Chicago Amphitheatre near the old stockyards on Chicago's South Side, or in the Chicago Stadium on the city's then prosperous near West Side. It was sponsored by a populist, even right-wing, Hearst-owned newspaper of the day, the *Chicago Herald-American*. John Schleppi of the University of Dayton has argued that the tournament rescued pro basketball from near-oblivion in the 1940s. "Professional basketball was in disarray in the late 1930s due to poor financial backing, quixotic leadership and the effects of the Depression," Schleppi wrote. "Against this background entrepreneur Harry Hannin and Leo Fischer of the *Chicago Herald-American* promoted the World Tournament of Professional Basketball which began in March 1939. Attracting the best available teams, they included the leading black and integrated teams. This was the first time blacks competed with whites on an even footing for a professional team championship. Using major facilities including the Amphitheatre and the Stadium, attention was drawn to the game during the war years."[1]

It was a valid tourney and drew up to 15,000 spectators per game, particularly at Chicago Stadium. The historic building with massive barrel vault roof served as the home of the Chicago Bulls until it was demolished in 1994; Michael Jordan played many of his professional home games inside it. The referees at the world tourney always were topflight, according to Schleppi, which addressed a chronic complaint against pro basketball officiating in the early days of the sport, namely that it was no good (for example, Jimmy Enright had been a referee during the 1944 competition). The World Professional Basketball Tournament was an important event, disappearing only after the merger of the National Basketball League and Basketball Association of America in 1949.

Fourteen teams competed in Chicago Stadium that March. The *Herald-American* began daily coverage of the event early in the month, announcing that Hartford and Dayton were late entries in the competition to complete the field.[2] Some previously selected teams, such as the Fort Wayne Zollner Pistons, Chicago American Gears, and Oshkosh (Wisc.) Stars simply came from the National Basketball League, which was heavily midwestern in orientation and mostly had its roots in former industrial league teams, such as Chuck's old Akron Firestone Non-Skids. Fifty teams from the Midwest and East Coast applied to play in the 1945 tournament, and the organizers always sought other nationally known teams, including so-called Negro squads. The timing of the World Professional Basketball Tournament typically meant it vied for attention with the more popular collegiate NIT (National Invitational Tournament), which was held in New York City during late

March each year. The NIT at one time was more popular than the NCAA Tournament and Final Four, but that has not been the case for decades.

The Chicago press made only passing reference to Dayton player-coach Colburn, a 5-foot-8 guard from Ohio State University and a high school coach, or to Gardecki, who had been a tool and die maker in Wilmington, Delaware, originally recruited to Ohio to play for an industrial league team sponsored by Frigidaire. Other regular-season Aviators were shown on a published roster, but they never went to Chicago. (Air-Tec Johnny Schick, though, had played professionally with the Aviators prior to being drafted, so his second tour with the team could be construed as a homecoming of sorts.)

The great "Negro" teams such as the Rens and Globetrotters received good press, and the Fort Wayne Zollner Pistons were lauded almost daily, and the reason was clear. Not only were the Pistons the defending tournament champs, but the National Basketball League standings published in the March 6 sports pages showed that Fort Wayne led the NBL Eastern Division with a 25-5 record. The next-best record in either division belonged to Dutch Dehnert's Sheboygan Redskins team, atop the Western Division at 19-11.[3]

The idea of "padding" a team was not overtly mentioned in the press, but it existed. Dehnert, coach of the 1941 world champions, had literally created a team in 1944 called the Brooklyn Eagles for the express purpose of competing in the tournament that year. The Brooklyn Eagles were made up of players from several contemporary pro squads, including Chuck Connors, who later played professional baseball and starred as TV's "Rifleman" in the 1950s, and Jack Garfinkle, who was in the Army at the time.[4] For the 1945 tournament, newspapers reported that the Pistons were to be joined by "Johnny Sines, former Purdue ace, and Frank Baird, former

Butler star," though neither ever show up in a box score from the Pistons' three clashes in the tourney.[5] Another article noted that three University of Wisconsin stars, including Des Smith, the Badgers' scoring leader, would join Oshkosh.[6] "Pop" Gates, a legendary member of the New York Rens, would play with the mostly white Long Island (N.Y.) Grumman team, as mentioned earlier. "Wee" Willie Smith, who had integrated the Acme Aviators during the regular season, was back with the Rens, also as noted earlier.[7] Maybe it was just musical chairs.

Favorites Fort Wayne and the Harlem Globetrotters drew byes in the first round, and early winners included the Aviators, who crushed the Long Island Grumman Hellcats, 43-27. Mahnken, Hansen, Light, Negratti, and Schick all were rostered, and another player, previously unknown, also got in the game—"Bob McNeil."[8]

A careful reading of every tournament basketball story in the *Herald-American* in March 1945 finds no mention of the Air-Tecs, however, or of Chuck Taylor. Even *Herald-American* featured columnists Jim Enright and Leo Fischer—contributors to the Converse Basketball Yearbook who clearly knew Chuck—were silent on the subject. Why? There are a couple of possibilities. Maybe they didn't know. Maybe. Another is that folks who knew simply acted to protect the Wright Field players. While the Dayton papers were careful to reiterate that the team members all were taking "furloughs" to travel to Chicago, it might still have raised eyebrows in the Windy City if it had been known that a bunch of soldiers somehow were not defending their country or not otherwise occupied on base. The *Dayton Herald*, however, impudently called the team the "Acme Air-Tecs" in several stories datelined Chicago.[9]

Or perhaps it was a matter of point shaving, point spreads, and "ringers" (superior players who really weren't supposed to be on your squad). Gambling on sports was nothing new —witness baseball's "Black Sox" scandal of 1919 when several Chicago White Sox stars were accused of throwing the World Series that year because of gambling payoffs. Basketball was no different. Remember Chuck's high school championship run, also in 1919? The Richmond, Indiana police chief had warned of gambling during the high school tourney and had promised dire consequences for anyone caught. A major college gambling scandal erupted in January 1945 when police cornered two Brooklyn College basketball players in the Brooklyn apartment of two gamblers (Henry Rosen and Harv Stemmer) and arrested the latter for conspiring with the boys to throw an upcoming basketball game against the University of Akron in the Boston Garden.[10] An even bigger point-shaving scandal was to break out at the City College of New York in 1951 that also involved the University of Kentucky. Eventually, seven teams and thirty-two players were to be implicated in a scheme that reportedly "fixed" eighty-six games during the 1950–51 season.[11] CCNY was coached by Nat Holman, the same man who allegedly helped Chuck land a job at Converse in 1921, and Kentucky was coached by Adolph Rupp, who was inducted into the Naismith Memorial Basketball Hall of Fame in 1969 as part of the same class as Taylor.

For Chuck, or Colburn, having a bunch of ringers on one team would certainly make for an attractive betting proposition—if you knew who the ringers were and the other bettors didn't. There is strong confirmation that gambling was in the air at the Chicago Stadium in March 1945. "In the second Dayton appearance an enterprising bettor could have had the Dayton team and four points against the Midland Dow Chemicals, while in the tussle with Chicago (American Gears) the betting fraternity was giving away 8 to 5 that the Acmes would be through," wrote a special correspondent for the *Dayton Daily News* who filed his dispatches from Chicago. John Wooden was to say years later that he believed Chuck would bet on golf games and the ponies, but thought he'd stop short of gambling on his own basketball games. But Wooden said that everything was not always on the up-and-up in basketball in those days. "I know sometimes in the old league (National Basketball League) when they had the three-game playoff the team that won the first game never won the second," Wooden said. "The way the money was divided they needed the third game. Was there any truth to that? I don't know."

The Aviators devoured the highly regarded Chicago American Gears in a record-setting 80-51 victory in the semifinals. A correspondent marveled at the play of Mahnken and Bob McNeil in particular and said the fans had taken a liking to these underdogs. "Even when playing the hometown Gears, Dayton was getting the most applause for its play. This situation stems from the fact that few, if any, know the Dayton players. The huge Chicago stadium is filled with spectators who want to know the answer to the question, 'Just who are these boys who are setting the best teams in the country on their ears?'"[12]

The bubble burst on March 24, a Saturday night, in the championship finale. The "Acme Air-Tecs" had traveled very far indeed, but the series ended in a blowout—the Pistons won 78-52 in front of more than 15,000 fans. The *Daily News* correspondent noted that each team got off about as many shots as the other, but more Piston tosses actually went in the basket.[13] In an ironic twist, Wright Field Air-Tec player Ed Sadowski came off the Pistons' bench to drop in nine points for the victors. Piston forward Buddy Jeannette was voted most valuable player of the tourney, but it was little-known Bob McNeil of the Aviators who actually led all tournament scoring with seventy-seven points, according to all three Dayton newspapers. What a slight that must have been for the person who was arguably the best player during the tourney. Not only that, McNeil wasn't even selected to the tournament's first or second teams. Aviator/Air-Tec John Mahnken, however, was tabbed for the first team.[14]

It's all too odd. Who was Bob McNeil, really? This was not Ralph McNeil, who played for a time for the Air-Tecs and who continued to play at Wright Field the following season, when the Air-Tecs were renamed the Kittyhawks. Bob McNeil was neither a former college All-American, nor a future NBA player—every other true Air-Tec who played in Chicago that March was one or the other or both. In fact, "Bob McNeil" was really Bruce Hale, the future University of Miami head basketball coach. "The strange thing was that Bruce Hale was about to receive the award as the best player but he played under an assumed name and they ended up giving the award to Buddy Jeannette," Pete Ankney recalled with great clarity. While college eligibility concerns kept young Dike Eddleman and Roy Witry away from the tournament, Hale had a bigger headache—he was absent without leave (AWOL) because he didn't have a furlough, as the other Air-Tec players did. He disguised himself so he wouldn't be thrown in the brig. Basketball historian Bill Himmelman got it right, though, in his box score for the 1945 championship game that accompanies Robert Peterson's *Cages to Jump Shots: Pro Basketball's Early Years,* where he simply lists Hale at forward instead of the mythical McNeil.

And so the lights went out for the season in the Chicago Stadium. In retrospect it seems like a children's story, a yarn about a bunch of neighborhood kids running out to the local park and choosing up sides, then saying, "OK, you be the Pistons, and we'll be the Aviators." It was all so fanciful and fantastic and yet perfectly real.

Though the Aviators fell short, and Taylor's name never was mentioned by the Chicago press, he received equal billing with Colburn on the team's return to Dayton.[15] Once again he had come close to greatness on the hardwood court, and once again he had fallen short. First it was with the Bull Dogs in 1919, who stumbled on their way to the Indiana boys single-class championship. Then it was his Non-Skids, who fell short at the industrial league championship in Erie, Pennsylvania in 1921. In March 1945 he had had yet another chance to be a winner—a real winner, in front of a combined tournament attendance of more than 50,000—although he would have had to be satisfied with the accolade "power behind the scenes." But he was a winner nonetheless. If history matters, then history has proven that Chuck Taylor was a great, great basketball man.

"Me"

8.

John Wooden sat in a cramped den in his suburban Los
Angeles condominium where he has lived thirty years, in a
room crowded by an old sofa and recliner, at a desk buried
beneath mounds of correspondence, and just under a wall
plastered with photos of all his UCLA championship basketball teams. It's not that Coach Wooden dwells on the accolades
and all the old titles. It's just that this is how his late, beloved
wife Nell, a fellow Hoosier from southern Indiana he met at
Martinsville High School, decorated the room, and that is
how the room will remain until the end. Unseen in this living
history museum, though, behind several autographed leather
basketballs on one shelf and yet more trophies and other
mementos on another, are the indelible tracks of all the other

early Hoosier basketball legends that Wooden says enriched his life, and America's, because of their love for the game of basketball, such as Everett Case, Ward "Piggy" Lambert, Tony Hinkle, Charles "Stretch" Murphy, and many others. One of those men was Chuck Taylor, a man Wooden first saw when Chuck put on a little clinic for the Artesians—that was Martinsville High School's nickname, after a flowing well in the town—and the two men became fast friends years later, after Wooden moved to Los Angeles in 1948 and Chuck followed suit in 1950. The two lived mere blocks away from each other for seven years. "I had a lot of fun with Chuck," Wooden reminisced. "I think maybe we enjoyed being hicks from Indiana, small towns in Indiana. We were Hoosiers. We had a lot in common and I think we were more comfortable than we would be with a lot of others, whether it was other basketball coaches or people in other areas."

Coach Wooden made the transition from what basketball historians call the pre-modern era to the modern era of the game much better than did Chuck Taylor. Wooden had been a successful high school coach in Kentucky and Indiana, then at Indiana State University in Terre Haute. But his best years were at UCLA, where he led the Bruins to ten NCAA Tournament championships before his retirement in 1975. More than a father of the game, he became a kind of surrogate father to millions of Americans, basketball fans and ordinary citizens alike, for his modest lifestyle and humble words, his salt-of-the-earth background, and a consistently moral stance as expressed in several books he penned over the years.

Wooden grew up with the same hard-packed dirt courts and hand-stitched, out-of-round basketballs as did Chuck Taylor, and the same, antiquated center-court jump ball after each score, but he did not reside in the past, in that pre-modern era of ever-changing rules, bad officiating, and nonstandard court size. Chuck, on the other hand, never tried to escape the legend and myth he had carefully crafted over the years. In so doing, Chuck let himself become a dinosaur.

The modern era in basketball is broadly described as the post–World War II period. More specifically, it dates from the rise of the National Basketball Association (NBA), which formed in 1949 out of the merger of the older but largely Midwest-based National Basketball League and the upstart Basketball Association of America, which was formed in 1946. The BAA was run by a group of metropolitan arena managers who wanted to promote attractions on evenings when their usual clients, ice hockey teams, were not playing home games. After substantial bloodletting for three years, in which four NBL teams simply jumped to the new league, the two leagues merged.

The modern era in the NBA can be dated in two other ways. First, there was the introduction of the twenty-four-second shot clock in 1954, which meant teams could no longer stall indefinitely to protect a lead. That same year, the "penalty shot" was introduced. This meant that teams fouled more than five times in a period received a bonus free throw attempt. The new rule was intended to cut down on intentional fouling and to speed up the game.[1]

Then there was the not-insignificant matter of television. Though the first basketball game was televised from Madison Square Garden in 1940, few people saw it. But early TV contracts in the 1950s were critical to making new stars in real time to a burgeoning audience. The public no longer needed to meet an "Original Celtic" or the father of the basketball shoe from the pre-modern era of the game; they were discovering a generation of new icons. If Chuck Taylor was to do any TV appearances in the 1950s, it would be on "What's My Line?" His trick shots and quick passes would barely qualify for a spot on "The Ed Sullivan Show."

Still, the Los Angeles years were the most promising in Chuck Taylor's life from a personal point of view, as well as the most disappointing. Chuck was coasting on his past glory—"He was content," Wooden says—and he was slowing down, doing fewer clinics, trading in royalties for a fixed income, playing golf where they played golf twelve months a year, hobnobbing with a new crowd of sophisticates in Hollywood, and taking in an occasional basketball game at UCLA or USC or Loyola Marymount. Wooden says his gym door was pretty much open to Chuck all the time. Taylor occasionally would try to pass on to the young Bruins the secrets of his trick shots and passes, which typically caused Wooden to blanch. Once, he sought to teach the Bruins an especially nasty old-time trick. Chuck would hold the ball between his hands, but high, in front of a player's face, then push it in suddenly, as if he were going to smash the ball in the boy's face, which invariably caused him to blink. That's when Chuck would make his pass—when the kid blinked. Wooden said he never liked that trick, and he warned his players that if he ever saw one doing it during a game he'd sit him down at the far end of the bench for the duration.

Chuck was full of tricks. He once designed a weighted basketball shoe that he convinced Dean Smith to use at North Carolina, at least prior to conference play in the ACC in the early 1960s. The theory was that the extra weight would make the boys quicker when they put on their regular All Stars, the same logic baseball players use when they swing weighted bats in the on-deck circle. But Smith said all his players suffered leg sprains while wearing the weighted shoes and Chuck soon abandoned the concept. The trial period for the weighted shoes was recalled by coach Larry Brown in 2004, when he threatened to make the U.S. Olympic basketball squad members practice in weighted shoes in an effort to improve their game, just as he had once done back at the University of North Carolina.

Chuck also would take gentle and not-so-gentle jabs at legendary coaches of the day just for fun. He once dared to tweak Adolph Rupp, the Kentucky coach, for not being more successful than he was! Rupp's won-lost record at Kentucky was 879-190, which most people would call successful, but not Chuck.[2] Chuck said Rupp only won big because he allegedly was the first coach in his conference to offer athletic scholarships, and he only beat other good teams because he insisted on playing them in Lexington. "Your winning percentage should be even better," he once chided Rupp, who did not take kindly to the taunts.[3]

Chuck knew how to have fun on and off the court, and he could insinuate himself into a gaggle of any famous basketball men at a Final Four or a dinner honoring this or that sports legend. Indeed, as Taylor turned over the clinic duties to younger, more vigorous men such as Joe Dean, Bob Davies, and Johnny Norlander, he seemed to increase his presence at conference finals, banquets, and even company dinners back in Massachusetts. But he was in the background. "It wasn't like a Dr. J or Larry Bird," recalled former Converse executive Bob Steenson. "People didn't seek out his autograph."

Los Angeles was Chuck's first true home as an adult. The house in Columbus simply was where his parents lived, though it had been his part-time residence and business address. Why did Chuck Taylor settle in Los Angeles? It was because he met a fading Hollywood starlet on a cruise ship bound for Hawaii in 1950, where he was scheduled to host a series of basketball clinics that year. Chuck did fewer clinics in the '50s overall, but he increasingly traveled farther afield to do them, including an Air Force tour across Europe in 1956 and a lengthy, well-documented goodwill tour to several South American countries in 1957 at the behest of the State Department. Ruth Alder had played the part of a dancer in *Bringing Up Baby,* a

1938 romantic comedy starring Katharine Hepburn and Cary Grant, and she was a telephone operator in 1941's *Design for Scandal,* starring Rosalind Russell and Walter Pidgeon. By the 1950s, Ruth, a small, dark-haired woman with sharp features, was working in the script department of one of the major studios. She and Chuck were married before a justice of the peace in Carson City, Nevada on May 26, 1950, and the happy couple settled in an upscale hacienda on Bellagio Road in Los Angeles, where they lived together for five years prior to their separation in 1955 and eventual divorce. He was forty-nine; she was forty-four.

"I think she thought he was rich," said Joe Dean. "He wasn't rich, but he lived a very nice lifestyle. He married Ruth, but it didn't last. The story was she had him followed all over the country and after three months she found something. He had women everywhere, you know."

Chuck's intentions in the marriage have to be considered earnest, though. He took Ruth on one swing out east to the increasingly important Carolinas and the Atlantic Coast Conference, where he introduced her to wartime friends Jimmie and Tassie Dempsey. Chuck's parents were deceased by then, but he stayed close to the Dempseys throughout the remainder of his life. The Dempseys clearly had become Chuck's second family after they settled near Raleigh following the war. Chuck spent many Christmases with the Dempseys and their children in Wilson, North Carolina (the kids called him "Pap"), and he told Tassie to charge the kids' All Star shoes at a local sporting goods store, where he always picked up the tab. Chuck introduced Ruth to the Dempseys on a swing through North Carolina, but she failed to impress. Tassie just remembered that Ruth's blonde dye job was garish at the time, and her whole body language was off-putting.

Chuck took Ruth to games at UCLA too, and he introduced her to all the fellows from Converse. "They lived together and traveled together," said Grady Lewis. "But no coach accepted her. She was an outcast. She was aloof. She just wasn't a warm person." For her part, Ruth threw many parties for her Hollywood cronies at home. But the marriage was in trouble from the beginning. She knew Katharine Hepburn and Cary Grant. Chuck knew "Phog" Allen and "Hank" Iba.

Still, they tried to make it work—Ruth didn't file for divorce until 1955, and it wasn't finalized until 1957. Chuck built a home office in his den in Los Angeles that was dominated by an overstuffed easy chair, a large desk smothered under appointment calendars and order forms, and a small rack for his collection of genuine briar pipes. He rarely drank—there were no whiskey or gin bottles about. Oddly, he kept no mementos, awards, or souvenirs from his early barnstorming or later coaching days on display. If Chuck really lived in the past, it was only a marketing ploy. Chuck Taylor—the man as opposed to the signature—was beginning to live in present bliss.

Yet Chuck's private life wasn't working. Wooden said Chuck fell in with a Hollywood crowd, mostly a "B" list of his wife's present and former associates. They were all bit celebrities, and so was Chuck by this time. John Wooden, on the other hand, who attended several of the soirees at Chuck's behest, was a rising star. Wooden says he was always glad to be with a fellow Hoosier from southern Indiana and talk shop (read: basketball), sometimes off in Chuck's office while the wine and champagne flowed into crystal glasses on the floor below, but he eventually tired of it. Wooden recalled a time Chuck twisted his arm a little, insisting that the coach allow a Hollywood friend to sit on the bench during a UCLA Bruins home game. "I let him sit on the bench," Wooden said. "Chuck had arranged this. After he had been there that night he wanted to pick me up and take me for lunch and he said he wanted to thank me—'You know how much I wanted to do that'—and he said, 'Now, you know I want to do something for you.' And I said no, I'm happy I was helpful to you, to do something you enjoy. He said, 'No, that's not enough. I have to do something for you. You know that little home you live in? You ought to do better than that. I have all sorts of money and I'd like to buy you a place or build it. Get your little woman and we'll find something very nice. I'll get you a nice car. What you're driving is a little Chevy; you should be driving something better than that. I'll get your wife something.' He said he had to do something. He wrote a check—'You fill out whatever amount you want.' I tore it up. He just couldn't get over that."

In time, Wooden stopped coming over to the Taylors, and Ruth stopped coming over to Chuck. The divorce took two years to play out, and the final decree for divorce was entered on March 12, 1957. She got the home on Bellagio, one of Chuck's cars (a Buick), $5,000 up front, attorney fees, and a large maintenance agreement. An apartment building Chuck owned in Los Angeles, valued at $60,000 in 1955, also stayed with Ruth. (Chuck's surviving friends say he was most bitter about losing the apartment, not the home.) But Chuck took care of his older brother, Howard E. Taylor, who had been injured during World War I. Money for his support would come off the top of the settlement, and should Chuck die before Ruth, she was to continue the payments to Howard.

Chuck griped that Ruth simply had the better lawyer, but in truth she had the goods on him. The lawsuit was clear: "Plaintiff is informed and believes and upon such information and belief alleges the fact to be that the defendant committed adultery with various persons on or about and during the period between January, 1954 and March, 1955 in the cities of Chicago, Illinois, San Francisco, Santa Monica and Los Angeles, California, and divers other places and lived in adulterous intercourse and committed adultery during said time with persons unknown to the plaintiff."[4]

Ruth went so far as to subpoena an executive secretary for the Converse Rubber Company's Chicago office, who knew how much Chuck really was making, before the estate was carved up. She subpoenaed everything. "I got taken," was all he could tell his friend Wooden after the ordeal.

They say it's good to travel when you're down in the dumps. Get outside yourself; see the world, how other people live; forget your troubles and all that. That may be what motivated Chuck to do the most extensive traveling of his life in 1956 and 1957, just as his heartache over a failed marriage was playing out in Los Angeles. He made goodwill visits to seventeen Air Force bases at home and abroad in 1956, and went on a well-documented, whirlwind trip across South America for the U.S. State Department in 1957.

The South American trips in particular not only spread the gospel of basketball abroad, but they were filled with love for this gringo, the "Embajador del Basquetbol," as he was routinely hailed. Spanish-language newspaper clippings showed Chuck and his translator, Felicio Torregrosa, a respected Puerto Rican educator, being hosted by officials from this or that ministry of sport, or working with both men's and women's teams, and quoted him extensively hammering away at the fundamentals of the game—blocking, screening, dribbling, passing, shooting, ball handling, and footwork. U.S. State Department dispatches also noted the warm reception Señor Taylor received everywhere he went—200 people here, 400 people there, and so on.[5] Customers for his shoe? Not really—Chuck had signed a waiver before the trip promising not to engage in any business for Converse whatsoever. But he was making friends for America, and that's what mattered to the State Department.

In one interview Chuck predicted that Brazilian basketball players could become the best in the world—if they practiced more discipline—and he knocked special coaching "systems" more directly than he ever had in print in the United States.

"NO MÁS DIAGRAMAS Y PIZARRONES . . . 'Pasó el tiempo en que los entrenadores utilizaban diagramas y pizarrones para hacer jugar basquetbol de memoria' dice Mr. Taylor."[6]

"NO MORE CHARTS OR BLACKBOARDS . . . 'The time when the coaches used charts and blackboards to make their teams play by memory is gone,' says Mr. Taylor."

Back in America, with the final divorce decree only days away in March 1957, Chuck made one of his regular stops at the NAIA "small-college" basketball tournament in Kansas City. Chuck attended every NAIA convention and playoff for years. Bob Davis, former men's basketball coach at Georgetown College and Auburn University, says sometimes Chuck spoke at the annual banquet and that he always had a storeroom open at the Municipal Auditorium and nearby Aladdin Hotel where coaches could gather to chat, get some free coffee, and, in a pinch, get some replacement shoes.

"He knew exactly how to talk to you," said Davis. "If you got beat you'd go in and he'd say, 'OK, you got beat but you looked pretty good. Keep your head up.' He was very encouraging to the young coaches."

To this day, the NAIA presents a Chuck Taylor Most Valuable Player Award at its annual tournament. Founded in 1940, the NAIA's main purpose was to promote basketball at the small-college level, and by the 1950s and 1960s it had expanded to include other sports such as track and field and even volleyball. Completely segregated at first, the NAIA tournament opened its doors to its first black player in the late 1940s (a second-team guard on Wooden's Indiana State University Sycamores, in fact), then to historically black Tennessee A&I College in 1953. The latter school won the tourney outright in 1957.[7] Tennessee State (as the school was later named) was coached from the 1953–54 season on by future Hall of Famer John McClendon, who had a personal bond with Taylor and even worked for Converse for a time after Taylor hired him on as part of the promotions department.

Tennessee State, under McClendon, was invited to an NAIA tournament in Kansas City during Christmas break 1954. McClendon was eager to compete, but Taylor told him he should accept the invitation "only if Tennessee State was allowed to stay in the same hotel and eat in the same restaurants as the tournament's other teams. Otherwise, McClendon's team would be at a psychological disadvantage," Taylor said.[8]

Chuck liked what he saw on the Tennessee team in 1957. That year's NAIA championship earned McClendon a featured spot in that year's Converse Basketball Yearbook, where he expounded on the "two in the corner" offense. McClendon later was to coach the ABA Denver Rockets (1969–70).

Also at the 1957 championship was Eugene Kimbrell, the athletic director and former basketball coach at Westminster College in Fulton, Missouri, and a co-founder of the NAIA. So was his wife, Lucille, also known as Lucy. In time, Lucy was simply to run off with Chuck Taylor.

It was a scandal that reverberated decades later in tiny Fulton. "Gene Kimbrell was one of the giants of small college basketball in the 1930s, 1940s, and 1950s," William E. Parrish recalled. "In particular, he helped establish the MCAU, which was the conference linking all of the small denominational colleges during that period and was one of the founders of the NAIA, the small college equivalent of the NCAA. I am sure that he and Taylor became good friends through those channels, and he came to Westminster with Gene's auspices to put on a workshop for the MCAU members plus probably other small colleges around Missouri. . . . Lucy was probably ten years or more younger than Gene, and it was quite a shock when she left him for Chuck."[9]

By all accounts, Lucille was a poised, accomplished, and educated woman of the first order. Born in 1908 in Batesville, Arkansas, her rural roots must have suited Chuck well, yet her refinement and education may also have appealed to his vanity. She often gave spoken word recitals and readings of important British and American poets.[10]

Lucy's son Alan, doing his military training at the time in San Antonio, was stunned by the turn of events. "I accept without question, nor need or desire for explanation, that you have not been happy with [my father] for the past few years," he wrote on hotel stationery. "I am certain that it goes deeper than you can or should tell me or anyone. I know that it must be quite strong to have led you to this stage."[11]

Eugene Kimbrell was struck low by the affair, though he did not publicly speak out about it or condemn Lucy. He eventually remarried and moved to Phoenix, and Lucy kept almost no evidence of his existence or her life with him in her home in Port Charlotte in later years. Faculty and staff at William Woods College also tried to come to terms with Lucy's decision to leave the college and Eugene. Several letters from R. D. "Randy" Cutlip, office of the president at William Woods College, express regret at Lucy's final decision to leave for good. "I will certainly understand if your decision is not to return but it will not be the same around here," Randy wrote on June 6, 1962. "You serve such a wonderful role in the faculty by quietly saying the right thing at the right time and you know no one could take your place with the students for they have such confidence in you and your judgment."[12]

Lucy spent some time in Evanston, Illinois in the late 1950s, to study with Wallace A. Bacon at Northwestern University, but also to be nearer Chuck who still had an office in Melrose Park. She also made at least one oral presentation at William Woods in early 1961, so the decision to leave for good must have been tortured and drawn-out. She sojourned in Baton Rouge, Louisiana between 1961 and 1962 and earned a master's degree there, but Joe Dean explained the real reason Lucy moved south.

"She didn't settle here," Joe said. "It was a very temporary thing. Chuck Taylor in those days was friends with virtually every coach in America. Of course, I lived here. I worked for Converse for some time and he felt that would give her somebody to lean on in case of problems. It was just to give her time."

Lucy Kimbrell and Chuck Taylor were married by the Rev. William H. Herring in Reno, Nevada on December 11, 1962, and the ceremony was witnessed by Helen and Link Piazzo.[13] Link, a shoe store owner who founded "The Sportsman" in Nevada in 1938, said Chuck drove to town one day with his bride-to-be, obtained a wedding license on the spot, and asked him to arrange the ceremony quickly, which Link did. "Chuck was divorced, you know," Link said. "The second time he was married he called me and said he wanted me to be best man. He wanted the wedding to be in Reno. I invited about 8 or 10 guests to be with him. I had it in a hotel. He was so appreciative of that."

Chuck was so proud of his new wife that he also took her "home" to meet his second family, namely the Dempseys back in Wilson, North Carolina. This time the reception and the impression were far different than had been the case for Ruth Alder. "He called us to tell us he was married," said Tassie. "We were all so excited. The moment we saw the car drive up Jimmie and I and the four children ran up to meet him. I think he wanted our approval."

Chuck's active role with the company waned in later years. He was sixty-one when he put his down payment on a golf course home in Port Charlotte, Florida in 1962, and he spent much more time on the links than on the hardwood in that decade. Don Williams, the former golf pro at the Port Charlotte Golf Club, played almost daily with Chuck for years. "I don't think he ever mentioned his basketball days," Williams recalled. "He was just another golf player. He was a 9–10 handicap."

Chuck and Lucy lived in a Master's Cup home, the costliest in the golf course community (the price was $25,000 in 1962, which included "optional" air conditioning). Almost all of Port Charlotte's subdivisions are built on subtropical wasteland. A series of narrow canals crisscross the section of town where Chuck and Lucy settled, but most lead nowhere—the dirt from the canals simply had been used to build the pads for the houses, which have no basements. General Development Corporation, the company that flew people in to a hotel near Port Charlotte and showed prospective customers models but not the actual tracts of land, charged more to live on one of those canals. Williams doesn't recall sale prices for empty lots, but the promotional campaign always read $10 down and $10 a month for a piece of land. Yet investors needed years before they could recoup their investment. Chuck picked a lot on the green at the first hole on the golf course, yet even his four-bedroom home was informally valued at a mere $100,000 after Lucy died in 2003.

"When we moved into this house, I started to unpack

his bags and he asked, 'What are you doing?'" Lucy told a reporter in 1996. "I said, 'I'm unpacking your bags,' and he said, 'Honey, I don't ever unpack my bags.'"[14]

Though Chuck continued to travel a bit in the 1960s, his life was on those links. He parked his golf cart outside his sliding patio doors in the evening, then jumped on it the next morning in anticipation of one or two more rounds of golf. He played golf like some people do their daily prayers. "I always remember Chuck had a Cushman gasoline golf cart," Don Williams recalled. "He was a little older and he didn't hit the ball as far as he used to. He'd hit it about 200 yards. Then he'd jump in his cart and drive off while you were trying to make your own shot. It was noisy and smelly and you just had to wait."

The best record of Chuck's later years comes from several diaries his wife kept that documented occasional clinics and sales calls, plus various awards banquets he'd attend. Visits to famous coaches, especially John Wooden and his wife, Nell, in California always were chronicled, but the entries generally were mundane—"had breakfast at The Madonna Inn," or "dinner at Lowery's"—plus constant admonitions from Chuck to just "put it on expense," fill most pages. Occasional car trouble was another favorite item—Chuck would fulminate over such things, but Lucy would just remain divine. Once, the happy couple was halfway to Georgia when Chuck realized he forgot to stow his golf clubs, so he turned around and headed back down the Gulf Coast to Port Charlotte to get them before continuing on his journey.

It's all innocuous stuff. But strains in the relationship show up several times, at least early in the marriage. Chuck was easygoing with all his business partners, but he practiced a kind of passive-aggressive style with Lucy at times. He never struck her or publicly humiliated her, but he often made her feel small. Chuck was uninterested to the point of being secretive in speaking to Lucy about his past, and though she was to gain a reputation as a knowledgeable basketball person over the years, it's clear Chuck never stooped to teach her the fundamentals. "The line between 'kidding' and making fun is very fine," she noted in one diary entry. "Nothing seems to give Chuck as much pleasure as catching me in a mistake. I guess smugness is as hard to live with and respond to positively as any of the minor vices."

Chuck's demeanor toward Lucy was to become a recurring theme in this diary. "Chuck resents any suggestions concerning taking care of himself—and he must have great need to prove himself always right, especially in small things—and he must need for me to be perfect for I'm constantly corrected. Perhaps having corrected boys for so many years I am a substitute."

This friction does not show up in later diaries dating from 1965 on, though, and Lucy was to treasure her few, short years with the shoe legend as evidenced by her abiding admiration for the man, even after the deaths of her other two husbands. Three years after Chuck's death in 1969 she married a man named Frank Hennessey, who himself had been married four times previously, and the two lived together for twenty years in the home that Chuck built. But Lucy's personal nurse said she believes the marriage never was consummated, and Lucy kept old letters from Chuck, plus a pair of his size-10 white high-tops in a box in her separate bedroom.

For the most part, Chuck and Lucy got along swimmingly. The first year of marriage may have represented a period of adjustment for the erudite Lucy and the laconic Chuck once they began living together full-time. He wrote many adoring notes to his second wife in the 1960s. The notes were bland, not much different than Lucy's diary entries, and almost always talked about what he had for breakfast, or described a golf game, or recounted yet another trip to a car dealer. Chuck almost always addressed his notes to Lucy as "Darling" and signed them with one word, "Me."

"Hi, Darling," begins one undated letter, written on Holiday Inn of Folkston (Ga.) stationery. "Report #1. Made my call with Fla. Sptg. and also checked the Lincoln Place in Bradenton. The price there was $2,000. (Undecipherable) Cad. In Tampa, their price was $1,700 which I thought was more like it. Lincoln don't have the same color as ours. Cadillac had a gold that is very close. Their car will be in Tampa very soon or before I get home. They are going to call me when it arrives.

"Now to get to the most important items. I love you. I miss you in the car. The room here is nice but you are not here. I just don't like to travel alone anymore. . . . All my love, Me."

Innocuous stuff, indeed. But Chuck Taylor had a few more cards to play in life, a few more windmills to tilt at, and one final curtain call to make before he departed the stage.

Glory

9.

Chuck Taylor, then in his sixty-eighth year, received many telegrams, congratulatory letters, and goodwill calls when he was inducted into the Naismith Memorial Basketball Hall of Fame in 1969. The letters and cards and telegrams were piled high on a circular table in the breakfast nook inside his Port Charlotte, Florida home. He could puff on the sweet-smelling tobacco in his briar pipe—he smoked that pipe all the time in his later years—or he might dip a small spoon into his favorite lemon ice cream and savor the fruits of his labors that had made his name famous all over the land.

One letter stood out. Chuck must have leaned forward on his elbows when he saw the postmark—it was from Terre Haute, Indiana—and a satisfied smile likely swept over his face as he unfolded the letter and read its contents. All the other correspondence from coaches and fans and businessmen were predictable, even "canned" accolades, but this piece of mail that he held firmly between his fingers was different. This was a tunnel back to his early career, a reminder to Chuck that he was so much more than a salesman or even an icon or just another retiree set out to pasture on a Florida golf course.

"My Dear Taylor," the letter writer began, then he noted the last time the two had seen each other. It was at a men's club in Indianapolis, possibly the toney Columbia Club on Monument Circle in the heart of the city, and he and Taylor had played "twenty-one." The letter writer, J. D. Clements of Terre Haute, chortled that Taylor had lost a small wager on the game. Then Clements got to the point.

"Duke Lovell asks me to ask you if you recall having brought a team here to play Jensen Bros. at the old Pennsy. Gym. He played on that team."[1]

Chuck remembered the game, the city, the gym, the times, the name; he could practically feel the vigor of youth in his arms and legs briskly take hold of him again. He remembered Duke Lovell, all right. Lovell, star shooter for the Jensen Brothers basketball squad, a superior semi-pro team of the era based in Terre Haute, had dealt Chuck Taylor and his traveling Converse All-Stars cage team one of its rare defeats during an otherwise magical season in 1926–27.

Chuck had been nominated for the Hall of Fame by long-time friend and native Hoosier Charles "Stretch" Murphy, who himself was a Hall of Fame member and former team-mate of John Wooden at Purdue University. In his later years Murphy was executive director of the Boys' Clubs of Tampa, not far from Port Charlotte. Murphy first nominated Chuck in a letter to Hall of Fame executive director Lee Williams in June 1968. "I feel, of course that [Taylor] is worthy of this top honor in basketball, or I would not be offering his name; that his life's work devoted solely to the promotion of basketball, giving thousands of clinics to hundreds of thousands of players and fans, starting the Converse Basketball Year Book, now in its 46th edition (copy enclosed), his poll (oldest in the country) and selection of All-American Teams, his staff, now made up of 11 men who he has trained, and who now give clinics throughout the country as he did for many, many years on his own and, last but not least, his developing what is considered (and has been since I can remember) the best basketball shoe in the world—to me this should more than qualify him for admission to the Hall of Fame as a Contributor."[2]

Chuck was in the shower when the phone call from Springfield reached Port Charlotte in 1969. Long-distance calls still were treated as urgent matters in those days. According to Gloria Schroeder, longtime nurse for Taylor's widow in her later years, the story was often told of how Chuck was smoking his pipe in the shower, with the water running down his neck and body, when Lucy came to tell him the news. He just walked out dripping wet and naked to the phone and took the call.

Chuck was in. Though surviving great coaches such as Ray Meyer, Red Auerbach, and John Wooden all attest to the validity of his selection as a "Contributor," questions have always dogged Chuck's selection. He was neither a great player nor a famous coach. He didn't always tell the truth, either. But he was in. There is another, more sinister hypothesis as to how Chuck Taylor got into the Hall of Fame as a "Contributor," though. To understand this alternate hypothesis, one has to know the relationship between the National Association of Basketball Coaches and the Hall of Fame. The NABC both proposed and underwrote initial construction of the original Hall of Fame in Springfield,[3] and Converse was a major financial backer of the NABC for years. Also, former Bloomington (Ind.) High School coach and fellow Hall of Famer Clifford Wells was the NABC executive secretary in the 1960s. Wells was the Indiana University undergraduate who coached Bloomington High School to the boys single-class championship in 1919, the year Taylor competed as a boy in the same tournament. Wells later coached at Chuck's old high school in Columbus in the 1920s, succeeding Chuck's friend Everett Case, who also briefly coached there, completing an amazing string of Hall of Famers with ties to the same small high school.

Wells was destined to write a moving eulogy for Chuck after Taylor's death in June 1969. He spoke about their youth together, not so much as close friends but as sons of the same soil, the same hills, the same earnest and nativist upbringing, then he got to the nub: "The N.A.B.C. is particularly proud that Chuck was a member of the N.A.B.C. He was one of the greatest boosters for this organization. He didn't win ball games, but he did win friends and he influenced people. Both coaches and players were recipients of his many acts of kindness. His was a big heart and many coaches got better jobs because he was a friend when needed."[4]

What Chuck mostly did for the NABC, however, was give it money, as documented in an earlier chapter. One might— just might—argue that Chuck Taylor's elevation to the Hall of Fame was payback for favors received.

Chuck could have been expected to bask in the glory of the limelight for a few days, then return to the sunsets on the long first green at his Port Charlotte home. One way or another, he had achieved the immortality he always sought via basketball. There was only one small problem with that retirement plan, however. With Chuck's glory days behind him, the great success of the Converse Chuck Taylor All Star shoe was about to unravel. It's true that the All Star sold well as a leisure and recreational shoe from the 1970s on, with tens of millions being sold to punk rockers, counterculture types, skateboarders, aging baby boomers, and young hipsters alike, and increasingly abroad, where the shoe became an endorsement of all things Americana. But the shoe expired as an important piece of athletic equipment in 1969. Johnny Wooden killed it. The most famous basketball coach in the nation, Wooden, every bit the sports guru that Knute Rockne and Vince Lombardi had been before him, decided his UCLA Bruins were not going to wear the shoe anymore.

"Even though my players wore them, I had to use a razor blade myself on every new pair to cut the seam that would be right over the little toe," Wooden told a reporter in 1987. "If I didn't do that, the players would all have blisters."[5]

Adidas, Puma, Reebok, eventually Nike—especially Nike —all came on the scene by the late 1960s not to praise Converse, but to bury it. Chuck Taylor was about to be steamrolled, and John Wooden decided to take the A train to the future. Other coaches and teams already had given up on Converse, either out of preference for the newer leather imports, or because they were paid to do so, but Wooden was a holdout until 1969.

Converse was dumbstruck by the rumors that Wooden might abandon their shoe—it would be like Michael Schumacher and his Formula One racing team evicting Ferrari. An internal company memo[6] specifically warned that if Converse lost John Wooden, there would be a domino effect—the company would lose every other contract with important and not-so-important teams in the country. The dread they felt must have been palpable. Converse executives held what amounted to a war planning session back in Massachusetts—Grady Lewis, owner Steve Stone, and John O'Neil, longtime general manager of the company, were there. This wise council discussed the lack of progress with the company's own prototype leather basketball shoe (high production costs; came apart in hard competition) and they decided to play the only card left in the deck—Chuck Taylor himself. If Wooden wouldn't be loyal to a shoe he had worn all his life, maybe he'd be loyal to a fellow Hoosier he had known most of his life. The company put Taylor on the next plane from Tampa to Los Angeles and hoped beyond hope.

Chuck and John sat in Wooden's den and reminisced about the old days. Chuck was a great salesman who knew you always talk first about family or things back home, and Wooden was ever the cautious horse trader, the very measured man his father had made him, just as he has described in his autobiography. Chuck would jaw a little, Wooden would smile a faint smile and nod his head, or clasp his fingers gently but firmly. It was all to no avail. "I talked to Chuck about [the shoe]," Wooden recalled in 2004. "I said I don't think you're keeping up with some of these new shoes. I think some of these shoes are better and if you don't make some changes I'm going to change. Well, I changed shoes the year that Chuck passed away. The Converse people think to this day that if Chuck hadn't passed away I would have continued using the Converse shoe. But that isn't true."

Though Wooden decided to abandon Converse in 1969, the Bruins didn't actually take to the court in Adidas leather shoes until the 1969–70 season. It caused a sensation among Lucy Taylor's intimates—she received almost as many conciliatory letters about the loss of the shoe contract as about the loss of her husband—but at least Chuck never had to see his old friend in another brand with his own eyes. "I talked with Bobby Davies after the game for I, like yourself, was upset about the shoes worn by UCLA knowing how close Johnny and Chuck were," South Carolina coach Frank McGuire wrote her after the 1970 Final Four.[7]

Though the All Star continued its strong sales in the casual sneaker market and sporadic fashion revivals since, its place in basketball history was as dead as the double dribble. No competitive team in the country continued to use it much longer.

The year 1969 was an odd, magnificent, and bittersweet year in Chuck Taylor's life. The only thing he was really famous for in the public eye was no longer taken seriously by important basketball men, and his signature had been reduced to the status of a "Betty Crocker" or "J. C. Higgins" (the old Sears, Roebuck brand name) by then. But he was in the Hall of Fame. During the ceremony he stood on a podium posing for the photographers with a resolute expression on his face, always enhanced by that long, prominent jaw of his, yet with a mistiness in his eyes reflecting a knowledge that while he had become a basketball legend in his lifetime, he had not quite become *the* basketball great he had wanted to be when he left home at age seventeen. There was only one thing left to do. He died.

"I take a physical every year," Chuck told a newspaper columnist in March 1968. "The last time the Doc went over me with a fine comb. When he finished I asked him how I was doing. The Doc didn't pull any punches. He told me that he had never examined a man who had such a history of broken bones. You see, back in those early pro days, gentleness was not exactly a habit. 'Outside of all the things that are wrong with you, you are in good shape,' the Doc said. He told me he could find nothing wrong with the heart or something that was important. So I guess I'll keep on watching basketball and selling shoes. It would be pretty awful if I couldn't."[8]

But everything was not all right. His arteries were hardening; the plaque was thickening; his blood was tired. Chuck went on with his life as if nothing was wrong, but a silent killer was stalking him from inside, and he suffered a massive heart attack on June 22 or June 23 of the following year and died on June 23, 1969. Some reports say he had just returned from a clinic in Pennsylvania, while others suggest he died suddenly at home. Lucy wrote that he died in the hospital where he had been admitted for another matter. "I can only be consoled by the knowledge that he did not suffer," she told Naismith executive Lee Williams. "He ate ice cream and teased the nurses, and patted me and kissed me and reassured me. He wasn't even ill. It was a massive heart attack—just a minute. So he didn't have to be crippled or diminished in any way. And he did have a wonderful life—he thought he was one of the most fortunate men in the world."[9]

Lucy dutifully called all Chuck's old friends with the sad news, including executives at Converse and Nell Wooden in Los Angeles. Chuck is buried at Restlawn Memorial Gardens in Port Charlotte. A southern-looking cemetery, it's replete with heavy, sprawling live oak trees with small leaves and hanging Spanish moss, and stickiness in the air you can feel on your skin. His remains are in the mausoleum, near those of Lucy's mother, Bertha Lee (Raines) Suthard, who had settled into a house next door to Chuck and Lucy shortly after their marriage. Only a small group of people were present at the funeral, including Tassie Dempsey and her husband, Jimmie, who was a pallbearer. No one from Converse flew down for the memorial service—the death of the shoe was apparently more important than the death of the shoe salesman. The champagne from the Hall of Fame induction was barely stale, yet so few people came to the chapel at Restlawn for the ceremony.

"When he died, I kept waiting to see if there was something written in *Sports Illustrated* about Chuck's death," said Tassie, "and there never was anything."

Appendix:
The History of the Converse
Rubber Shoe Company

The Converse All Star shoe did not come about because of Chuck Taylor. He did not conceive it, create it, or produce it. Rather, it was the vicissitudes of a seasonal market for foul-weather rubber boots that inspired factory owner Marquis Converse to begin making canvas shoes in 1915, and by 1917 he added an all-purpose gymnasium shoe called the All Star. His company, originally called the Converse Rubber Shoe Co. (later renamed Converse Rubber Co., then Converse, Inc.) and based in Malden, Massachusetts, often sent its employees home for the winter once Christmas break began. Orders for galoshes were filled by then, and new orders would not pick up until the spring. As an internal Converse company history noted, "[m]anufacturing canvas tennis shoes helped to smooth employment seasonally by keeping workers busy when there was little demand for waterproof products."[1]

It's clear that the All Star was not the first "basket ball" shoe. Basketball historian Robert W. Peterson writes that A. G. Spalding & Brothers made a rubber-soled, canvas, high-top basketball shoe circa 1900, and his book reproduces an ad for it from 1904.[2] It looks like a cross between a men's wrestling shoe and a lace-up ladies' boot.

The market for a basketball shoe clearly existed before the All Star's appearance in 1917. Basketball was a growing sport, and physical education was a core American value, both for YMCAs and public schools. Other early basketball shoe manufacturers included Mor-Shu and Reach. The latter company made "Good fitting Basket Ball Shoes" and promoted them through their Reach Guides, which covered professional basketball from about 1902 to 1926. (Reach and Spalding both published basketball guides prior to the Converse Basketball Yearbooks, which began in 1922.) Additionally, Goodyear made the "Wingfoot" by 1921, if not before; the Akron Goodyear Wingfoots played in them exclusively.

Yet the rubber-soled, canvas-top shoe apparently was not created by any of these companies. According to Cameron Kippen of Curtin University of Technology in Perth, Australia, "[b]y the 1860s a croquet shoe was marketed which had a rubber sole with a canvas upper fastened with laces."[3] This was in England. Later in the nineteenth century, seaside "plimsoll" shoes also had rubber bottoms and canvas uppers. The term "sneaker" dates from this era, writes Kippen, because thieves allegedly preferred the rubber-soled shoes as it was easier to sneak about silently in them.

Kippen credits U.S. Rubber Co. and "Keds" with being the first rubber-soled, canvas-top "tennis shoe" in America, and says Converse's innovation was to make a Keds-type shoe in an ankle-high model. This is at some variance with what Peterson reports, but the role of the U.S. Rubber Co. should not be dismissed. According to Mary Bellis, U.S. Rubber sold their shoe under thirty brand names over the years. The shoe was almost indistinguishable from the All Star, save for a different, more vertical pattern on the front rubber bumper (All Stars have a diamond pattern in front).[4] Richard Lapchick, the son of Original Celtic Joe Lapchick, said his father endorsed the similar "Joe Lapchick Basketball Shoe," also known as "The Playmaker," exclusively for Kinney Shoe Stores for years.[5] U.S. Rubber Co. made it. (The Lapchick endorsement also dates from 1932, the same as Chuck's.)

The All Star was reasonably successful from its inception, but it was not a runaway best-seller until after World War II. Marquis M. Converse, who had previously operated a department store, opened his company with $250,000 in capital and fifteen employees in 1908. By 1910, the company was producing 4,000 rubber boots a day. The All Star came along in 1917. "Sales of the All Star were slow but steady until the late 1940s when interest in basketball surged," the Converse company history reports.[6]

Chuck Taylor was no more than a journeyman basketball player whose most famous team was the Akron Firestone Non-Skids, an important industrial league quintet. Yet he played for the team only during part of the 1920–21 season. His stronger association was with the Chicago-based Converse All-Stars basketball team in the mid-1920s. (The name of the shoe did not use a hyphen, but the team name did.) It was common for athletics manufacturers and sporting goods companies to sponsor their own basketball teams during this era. Indeed, Chuck played briefly for the Detroit Rayls, a sporting goods company team sponsored by T. B. Rayl Co. of Detroit. That Converse would name a basketball team after their basketball shoe seems an obvious choice. Taylor, the ex-pro (if not ex-star) was player-manager. It's known that Chuck's name was added to the shoe in 1932 because no Converse Basketball Yearbook through 1931 shows the well-known All Star ankle patch with five-point star in the middle of a circle and Chuck's signature. It shows up only in 1932, when Chuck also began promoting his college All-American basketball player list. Grady Lewis, a former basketball star and coach and

The History of the Converse Rubber Shoe Company

Converse executive, said however that Chuck's signature was added in 1931.

Marquis Converse lost the company in 1928 when it went into receivership. The failure was linked to an ill-fated effort to market an automobile tire, the "Converse Cord." This was a hard rubber tire at first, then a balloon tire beginning around 1925. Quality control problems and many "returns" doomed the latter, and the tire line was discontinued the same year the company went into receivership.

Mitchell B. Kaufman, president and owner of the Hodgman Rubber Co. in Framingham, Massachusetts, bought the company in 1929, and Marquis M. Converse died two years later. "Founder and Former Head of Converse Rubber Co. Dies of Heart Trouble at Wheel of Car on Milk St., Boston. Was Remarkable Salesman."[7] So read the headline on the front page of the *Malden* (Mass.) *Evening News* the day after Converse died.

The accolade "remarkable salesman" is not entirely gratuitous. Converse did not like selling to wholesalers or "jobbers." He had a sales team that marketed directly to stores, which inevitably led to the Chuck Taylor basketball clinics, which made Chuck a "demonstrator" in the great tradition of marketers in the early part of the last century.

A biographical sketch of Marquis Converse tells us: "A native of Lyme, N.H., he was born 70 years ago, the son of Peter Mills and Sarah S. Converse. He was educated in the country schools and Thetford, Vt., Academy. At 18 he went to Canada and learned telegraphy and a few years later returned to Boston and entered a large department store, rising to the position of superintendent. Ill health forced him to resign and he went to Lebanon, N.H., where he purchased a small department store."[8] The Malden, Massachusetts plant was built on Pearl St., an interesting coincidence in that Chuck Taylor ran

Appendix

his various small sideline businesses, such as knee pads and golf tees, from his home on Pearl St. in Columbus, Indiana throughout the 1930s.

In 1933 Converse Rubber Co. was purchased by the Stone family—Joseph, Harry K., and Dewey D. Stone. The family ran the business for the next thirty-nine years; Stephen Stone was the last in the line at the helm.

Converse had its best years under the Stone family, in part because the company's marketing strategy was good. It's no exaggeration to say that Chuck Taylor and later ex-athletes did the "fundamentals of basketball" clinics in front of millions of young athletes and fans well into the 1980s, teaching the game of basketball not only to America but to the world. The annual Converse Basketball Yearbook, begun in 1922 and expanded in 1929, also helped sell shoes by showing pictures of top college teams in the country wearing Converse shoes. The yearbook was eagerly awaited each fall by tens of thousands of fans until its demise in 1983. Any high school or college team could get its picture into the yearbook for free, as long as a majority of players shown were wearing Converse shoes! There were also regular payments reaching to $50,000 a year to the National Association of Basketball Coaches, including subsidizing the luncheons at the NABC's annual convention, which clearly bought loyalty for the company.

Former Converse executives speak well of Stephen Stone. "You couldn't have had nicer people than the Stone family," said former Detroit Piston and Hall of Famer Bob Houbregs, who began in the sales and promotion division of Converse with Chuck Taylor in 1959. "You didn't get paid a lot but they always took care of you."

"Very, very influential people in the state of Massachu-setts," recalled Bob Steenson, a longtime Converse employee and unofficial historian of the company, in speaking of the

Stone family. "They knew people, if you know what I mean. They were very well-respected."

During his life, Steve Stone sat on his local school board in Wareham, Massachusetts, continued the Stone Charitable Foundation that his father and uncles had established, and was awarded an honorary degree from Hebrew College. Stephen Stone died at age eighty-four on May 30, 2002. According to his obituary, "Mr. Stone was at the helm of Converse Rubber Co. for much of the All Star's heyday in the 1950s and 1960s. The vulcanized rubber and canvas shoe was the choice of 90 percent of college basketball players then. . . . In 1972 the Stone family sold Converse and he retired as president of the firm."[9]

The company was sold to New York–based Eltra Corporation in 1972. More significantly, the company purchased a relatively new manufacturing plant from rival athletic shoe manufacturer B. F. Goodrich in Lumberton, North Carolina that year as well. This factory had been making the P.F. Flyer, one of several competitors to the All Star. Converse already had branched out to other New England factories and to Puerto Rico, but the Lumberton plant was to be the most modern—and ultimately last—operating Converse plant in the country when it shut down in 2001. Converse also acquired the Jack Purcell tennis shoe in the deal. The Canadian-born Purcell was the world badminton champion in the 1930s and his namesake shoe was offered as a "court" shoe. Purcell also is credited with personally helping design the instep.[10] (Incidentally, actor James Dean indirectly was a Jack Purcell tennis shoe endorser in the 1980s. A successful marketing campaign years after Dean's death showed him in a relaxed moment on the set while filming *Giant;* he has his feet up, and he's wearing Jack Purcells. Converse officials said at the time that the ad campaign boosted sales of the brand by 30 to 50 percent.[11])

Converse had an important role during World War II, as did many American industries. The company made rubber protective footwear, rubber-coated parkas (you've seen these in countless historic photos and World War II movies over the years as GIs slosh through the French or Belgian countryside), and the shearling-lined A6 flying boot for the war effort. The company also mailed copies of an in-house publication, *Converselations,* to former employees serving overseas and bought large sums of war bonds. The workers' union also sent bonus checks and cartons of cigarettes to former colleagues who were now soldiers.

An article in the local Malden paper during the war touted "100 percent employee war giving," meaning that every employee directed at least 10 percent of his or her salary to war bonds or other savings schemes, over and above the company's substantial contribution. One headline declared, "Company announces purchase of $200,000 in Bonds, Fifth War Loan Drive. Employees average Twelve Percent."[12]

The company has kept hundreds of letters from GIs sent back to Malden during the conflict. "Dear Friends [of Local 22763 AFL]: I received your gift of a carton of cigarettes two days ago and I sure do thank you for your thoughtfulness. It makes a better soldier when someone on the outside is pulling for him." Signed, "Joe Paschal" and dated January 3, 1943.

"Dear *Converselations,*

"Was glad to receive my copy and check. I sure like to see it each month. It cheers me up a bit to see the old name again. . . ." Signed "ex-worker Bill B." Dated May 9, 1943, and mailed from Fort Sill, Oklahoma.

"I am now in the Third Army which means occupation work as long as we remain in it. We are about 15 miles from the Austrian border. I hope to visit there . . . soon which will add up to nine countries I have been in but give me the good old States any day." Signed "Joe" and sent in 1945.

The All Star shoe apparently was degraded during the war. Former DePaul University coach Ray Meyer said he couldn't stand the synthetic rubber sole the company was using in its shoe during the conflict. But he had connections. "During the war they were making all these synthetic rubber soles and they (Chuck Taylor and others) would send me the shoes with the real rubber soles. They were wonderful."

Converse Chuck Taylor All Star shoes had been slow to change in their early years. For example, "white" Chuck Taylors were introduced by Converse exclusively for the 1936 U.S. Olympic team, then rolled out for the general public the following year. The 1936 Olympics were the first that included basketball as an official sport. Yet it was the Olympics, so important to the company in 1936, that were to prove an early death knell for Converse in 1968, as Adidas and Puma leather shoes from Germany attained international stature at the Mexico City games that year. Some college basketball programs already had abandoned the canvas shoe in the early 1960s. John Wooden, Hall of Fame coach at UCLA for many years, announced he was abandoning the shoe in 1969, but did not do so until 1970, the year after Chuck's death. Within a decade, almost no school basketball team wore the canvas shoe, though the All Stars continued to sell well in the casual shoe market.

An internal Converse document in 1969 told of problems with the company's own leather shoe. "Our first production of the new Leather All Star, as it is presently designed, did not prove to be as successful as we had hoped. We encountered several problems in certain features on the shoe, in the performance of the shoe, and our method of manufacturing the shoe.

Appendix

These problems have temporarily forced us to stop production to allow us time to correct these problems. Our inability to produce these shoes as planned will delay our delivery schedule, particularly on dealer orders."[13]

Allied Corporation, a large chemical conglomerate, purchased the company in 1979, then spun it off in 1982 to senior managers at Converse for $100 million, and the company was renamed Converse, Inc. The company rolled out various padded leather All Star shoes and signed expensive endorsement deals with Julius Erving (1975) and Larry Bird and Magic Johnson (1979), and purchased the rights to be "the official athletic shoes of the Los Angeles 1984 Olympics" for $1 million. The company also began its own biomechanics lab for the express purpose of developing a competitive running shoe. The lab, the only one in America besides Nike's for a time, was to prove costly.

"In 1985, Converse unveiled a multi-million dollar, state-of-the-art biomechanics lab in their newly-built North Reading, Mass., headquarters,"[14] the internal company history reports. The lab developed mid-sole cushioning systems, energy return technology, and motion control devices. The technology went by the name of Energy Wave and Blue Wave for several years, but Converse running shoes never sold well.

Advertising budgets also skyrocketed, to $25 million annually by the mid-1980s. The advertising campaigns were reasonably successful, though the company could never match Nike's enormously successful deal with Michael Jordan dating from 1986. Converse played off the Larry Bird–Magic Johnson rivalry for several years, and in 1991 launched its most successful TV ad campaign, known as "Grandmama." This was 6-foot-7, 250-pound Charlotte Hornets forward Larry Johnson, who dressed as "Grandmama" and did slam dunks in full drag. Converse also introduced a "React" gel-packed shoe called the Run 'n' Gun in 1993, but after adverse publicity the name was changed to Run 'n' Slam.

The endorsement game bit Converse badly in the end. In 1990 Converse created a new thirty-second highlight film/advertisement of Magic Johnson's on-court accomplishments, then spent $10 million launching a Magic Johnson apparel line the same year. The next year, Johnson announced he was HIV-positive, apparently contracting the deadly virus from a prostitute. The clothing line was not successful. And Magic Johnson developed a propensity for bad-mouthing the company. "Converse as a company is stuck in the '60s and '70s," Magic told a group of reporters as the U.S. Olympic basketball team practiced in 1992. "I've been trying to get out for years."[15]

Magic repeated his complaints in a newspaper interview later that year, saying that Converse didn't promote him as heavily as Nike pushed Michael Jordan, and again he announced he wanted out of his $2-million-a-year contract.[16]

Converse was bit yet again by a shoe contract, this time with Latrell Sprewell, who was suspended from basketball for several months after choking Golden State Warriors coach P. J. Carlesimo during a practice in December 1997. Converse suffered terrible publicity and dropped Sprewell.

Then there was the colorful Dennis Rodman. Converse cancelled a $15 million shoe contract with him in 1999. "The whole idea was to use Rodman's obvious visibility to increase the numbers in the basketball shoe area—where sales are flat industry-wide—to try to solidify the core business while expanding into fashion and performance sneakers," Gregg Hartly, executive director of the Sporting Goods Manufacturing Association, told the *Boston Globe*. "It didn't work. Dennis was always in the spotlight more for his personality problems than what he did on the court."[17]

From roughly 1980 on, various Converse shoes carried the Chuck Taylor All Star label, including padded leather shoes made abroad that were competitive in terms of performance with modern shoes from Nike and Reebok, if not quite as popular. The new shoes cost a lot to develop and introduce, however, and the company lost money on several shoe lines. The original made-in-the-USA canvas Chuck Taylor All Star never ran in the red, however. They were featured in the popular 1986 film *Hoosiers,* starring Gene Hackman, and the shoes became a favorite of art students, the new counterculture, and the grunge rock music scene of the early 1990s. In recent years children in many ads and fictional characters on screen who are supposed to be hip, alternative, or "young" have been shown wearing the shoe, or a knockoff. The export market also expanded for the true All Stars, as the canvas and rubber shoe and trademark ankle patch became American icons (even though most of the canvas was made in Mexico in later years). In 1995, for example, 40 percent of the canvas shoe's sales were overseas.[18]

The company kept making business errors. In May 1995, Converse acquired Apex One, Inc. as a wholly owned subsidiary. Apex One designed and marketed activewear and sportswear under license from several professional sports teams and leagues, colleges, and universities, but was near bankruptcy at the time of the sale and was having delivery problems on new orders. "At the time of the acquisition it was believed that Apex would provide Converse with a complementary product line and entry into the licensed sports apparel sector, as well as offer the company a more competitive and strategic position in the industry."[19]

By August of the same year, however, Converse shut down Apex One. The company couldn't get many new orders, suppliers demanded payment up front, and Converse didn't want to fund Apex's debt further. The venture stuck Converse with a $41.6 million debt, more than half its losses for 1995.[20]

Converse also continued to undergo ownership changes

The History of the Converse Rubber Shoe Company

throughout this era. A St. Louis–based manufacturer, Interco, Inc., which also sold Florsheim dress shoes and Lane and Broyhill furniture, bought the company in 1986. But Interco filed for Chapter 11 bankruptcy in 1991, and Apollo Investment Fund gobbled up 60 percent of the stock. In 1994 Interco spun off Converse, and the new company was "controlled" by investor Leon Black. Converse dumped its unprofitable running, walking, tennis, and football lines the following year. In 2000 Converse rolled out a helium-cushioned basketball shoe, which failed to take off, and the company filed for Chapter 11 bankruptcy in January 2001.[21]

This bankruptcy was to be the proverbial last nail in the coffin for the company, though there was to be an improbable resurrection two years later. The sole surviving U.S.-based All Star factory, in Lumberton, North Carolina, closed on March 31, 2001, prior to the assets of the company being purchased by Marsden Cason and William Simon later that spring.

Nearly 500 workers at the plant were thrown out of work when the doors were shuttered. At its peak, the Lumberton factory operated multiple shifts and employed about 2,400 people. The assets were bought at auction for $117.5 million; the most interesting asset was Chuck Taylor's name. Cason and Simon had previously run The North Face, Inc., an outdoor adventure clothing manufacturer.[22] Converse headquarters was moved to rented space in a restored mill in North Andover, Massachusetts that employed fewer than 200 persons, and all manufacturing was done overseas, mainly in Indonesia and China. Converse, Inc. had become essentially a licensing and marketing company.

The closing of the Converse factory in Lumberton hit the community hard, raising unemployment levels to more than 10 percent by May 2001. The company had contributed $10.5 million in wages and $125,000 in taxes to the local economy even at the end. "It's been the mother to Robeson County and a lot of other areas," M. L. "Moe" Davis told a local newspaper on March 24, 2001. Davis had run a grocery store a mile from the Converse factory gates since 1953. In addition to the Lumberton workers, several hundred other Converse employees in Mission, Texas and in Mexico also lost their jobs at this time.[23]

Mable Moses, a thirty-three-year Converse employee, lost her job in March 2001, prior to the purchase by Cason and Simon. "I met my husband when he was working with Foot Locker in our mall in Lumberton, North Carolina," she wrote this author on March 14, 2001. "At that time, I had just started to collect tennis shoes as sort of a hobby and wore different pairs each day to work. I happened to be wearing a pair of metallic blue hi-top Chucks the day we met. He had taken a tour of our plant in Lumberton and I saw him then for the first time. He commented on my shoes and that was all she wrote. At that time I had about 100 pairs of Chucks in my collection. Since then and almost fourteen happily married years of marriage, my collection has grown to over 500 pairs. There's Chucks, Jack Purcells, Converse sandals, etc. The plant has been selling them like hotcakes to the remaining employees and I've been coming home with about five to six pairs every week." Moses later wrote that at age fifty-three, she was drawing unemployment benefits for the first time in decades and was hoping to go back to school to learn a trade for a new career, but she had no idea what that might be.

Converse, Inc. was sold yet again, in September 2003. This time Nike bought the marketing and licensing company for $305 million and announced Converse would operate as an independent business unit. The company was up to some of its old, ill-advised marketing tricks late that year as well. A new Converse basketball shoe called the Loaded Weapon was

The History of the Converse Rubber Shoe Company

introduced for the 2003–2004 season and endorsed by five young NBA players, but coaches across the country decried the name, which was highly reminiscent of the Run 'n' Gun debacle a decade earlier.[24]

The Nike purchase also irked anti-globalization groups. *Adbusters,* a British-based anti-globalization magazine, went so far as to schedule introduction of its own Chuck Taylor knock-off called the "Black Spot" sneaker in 2004. Made of canvas and rubber, it also featured a black spot about the size of the All Star's ankle patch, and the company promised that fair wages would be paid to employees.[25]

A less controversial Converse ad campaign launched in 2003 focused on Chuck Taylor, the man. Even though Magic Johnson belittled the historic connection, Converse began featuring the famous Akron Firestone Non-Skid rooftop photo of Chuck dating from 1921 on its Converse Chuck Taylor All Star shoe tags, and featured "Mr. Taylor" by name in hip-hop lyrics that accompanied some of its TV ads beginning that year. The song is catchy and the lyrics are hard to hear, unless you download them from a web site: "Before Mr. Taylor taught the world to play, before Fiberglas, before parquet, before the word 'doctor' was spelled with a J and ballrooms were ball courts where the Renaissance played."[26]

Betty Crocker and Chuck Taylor. Juan Valdez (the coffee bean guy) and Chuck Taylor. At least Chuck Taylor was real, more real even than the people who own his name realize. Yet the wonderful basketball yearbooks are gone. The "Made in USA" claim is gone. The Akron Firestone Non-Skids are gone. The "fundamentals of basketball clinics" and the Wright Field Air-Tecs and all the rest—it's all gone. But Mr. Taylor, who really did teach the world to play, has not quite altogether gone away.

Appendix

Notes on Research

Typically, when a scholar presents information that is contrary to previous knowledge and/or belief, an explanation is required. How did everyone else get it so wrong, for instance?

The ghosts of biographers past are not really scowling at me on this one, however. Chuck Taylor had no biographers. But there was a Converse, Inc. archivist, the Naismith Memorial Basketball Hall of Fame, Converse's own web site, and so on. Were they all wrong?

The reporting on Chuck Taylor had simply been reduced to the level of advertising copy writing in recent decades. Every recent newspaper column and every story on the Internet I found on Chuck was entirely derivative, meaning they just copied what someone else had written.

As always, primary sources were the key to this new narrative of Chuck Taylor's life. For me, that meant finding pre–World War II newspaper clippings and people still alive who personally knew Chuck as far back as possible. My big break came when I received an e-mail from a former employee of the Lumberton, North Carolina factory that was the last in America to make the Converse Chuck Taylor All Star shoe. She had written to tell me about her collection of 500 pairs of the shoe—all different styles—and how she was doing in an employment training program the state had sent her to. She was fifty-three at the time.

This woman also told me that Chuck Taylor's widow used to send her shoes. I immediately asked for the address. Maybe the widow was still alive. I obtained the address, but no phone number could be found. Several letters to an address in Port Charlotte, Florida went unanswered, so I had the idea to send a certified mail letter with return receipt. If my earlier letters were not being returned, that meant someone was picking them up. I received no response to my certified mail letter, either, but I was able to check the signature of the person who had picked it up.

It turned out to be the widow's full-time nurse, and I found *her* phone number on switchboard.com. The nurse had received all my letters and had forwarded all of them to the widow's son (Chuck's stepson; Chuck had no children of his own). I contacted the man and eventually was allowed into the widow's home to personally review all Chuck's extant papers and artifacts. I could not interview the widow, however. She had suffered a stroke several years earlier, was uncommunicative, and her son only let me into the home after she died.

Another break came when Converse, Inc. allowed me into *their* archives. I always felt that Converse, Chuck's longtime employer, had files on the man. Besides, I had found a letter from a Converse executive thanking Lucy Taylor Hennessey, Chuck's widow, for all the newspaper clippings and photos she had provided the company! I made several calls to Converse officials in 2001, to both the old and new management teams, and it was in July 2003 that I was granted access to the company's archives.

My best finding in North Andover was Aurilla Taylor's scrapbook with several dozen old newspaper clippings. None

Notes on Research

was dated; none had a dateline. They were just the barest newspaper clippings glued or stuck into an old leather-bound scrapbook, the kind tied along the spine with what looks like shoestring. How to date them? Where did they come from?

One clipping spoke of Chuck playing ball in Richmond and Seymour. Well, I knew that Richmond and Seymour were in Indiana. What year, though? I saw on the back side of one loose clipping from this same set an ad for a new 1927 automobile. It was fairly straightforward to search the Richmond, Indiana newspapers during the basketball season for 1926–27. From there, I found clues to other newspapers in other cities, and so on.

About 90 percent of my newspaper citations are fairly complete, and by that I mean they at least have title and date of publication, and most of those have headline, author, and page and column information, where appropriate. Some clippings remain undated or otherwise incomplete, however. I felt I had established my credibility by dating and naming most of the clippings, and a few (such as an article about Chuck's appearance in a golf tournament in the mid-1930s) were not important enough to continue the search for a better citation.

Uncovering Chuck's military history was difficult. One source had previously declared that Chuck was a coach during World War II on an Air Force base, but didn't know which one. I felt it had to be Wright-Patterson Air Force Base, which was the premier Army Air Corps base during the war, and I was right. Several people at the base were unhelpful at first, telling me I was wrong, refusing to look up old post newsletters they admitted existed, and denying me access to check for myself based on post–September 11 security concerns. Eventually, I found one newspaper clipping that specifically placed Chuck and his basketball team at Wright Field in December 1944, so I sent that off to the base as a kind of proof of what I was claiming. The clipping was forwarded to the base historian, who had never been told of my earlier search, and he was helpful. (He used my information as part of a base history he was writing for the government, going so far as to send me a proof of his copy and asking me to check it for accuracy.) I also journeyed to the Montgomery County Public Library in Dayton on my own, looked up several old newspapers, and found additional information in the library's vertical files.

All along, I was collecting names, names that were turning up in articles about Chuck. Were they still alive? Most were not. But through easily accessible online databases and asking surviving friends if they knew any additional surviving friends of Chuck, I was able to track down about twenty people who could give me firsthand information and anecdotes. Dean Smith, the retired University of North Carolina men's basketball coach, ignored my initial request for an interview. After I persisted, he finally called me back, laughed, and said he thought the original request must have been a mistake. Nobody had called to talk to him about Chuck Taylor in decades. Decades.

Other information came from public records. I saw from Chuck's insurance policy that he had been divorced prior to his marriage to Lucy Taylor Hennessey. With a date and names in hand, I wrote away for his divorce papers and from those tracked down a little information about his first wife, bit actress Ruth Alder. I also obtained Chuck's military identification number from a confidential source (someone who should not have given it to me because I was not a family member, but who wanted to help me anyway). From that, I was able to trace a thorough timeline for Chuck's military service up to and including his period at Wright Field. I also traveled to the National Archives and Records Administration II in College Park, Maryland to seek out records on the Army's

Notes on Research

Special Services Division (worth a book or dissertation in its own right), and I hired an outside researcher to look up State Department records for me at a later date.

It was my personal quest. I felt like one of those guys on public television who jumps on an old steam engine in a third-world country in search of an ancient civilization and a great story to tell. It was a great adventure for me. It was more fun than the writing of the book itself.

Notes

Introduction

1. "Commercials Take Game From Soldiers: Game Was Fast and Interesting and Final Score was 45-30; Concordia Defeats Em-Roes," *The* (Columbus, Ind.) *Evening Republican,* March 20, 1919, page number unknown.

2. Bob Sherrill, "Where is Chuck Taylor: His Name Lends Status To A Popular Basketball Shoe," *Durham Morning Herald,* Feb. 2, 1981, p. 11-A.

3. John Hughes, "The Myth Behind the Shoe," *Orange County Register,* Feb. 8, 1997, p. D-1.

4. Ibid.

1. Hall of Fame

1. Chuck Taylor to Lee Williams, director of the Naismith Memorial Basketball Hall of Fame, Springfield, Mass., June 7, 1969.

2. Edna Thayer, retrospective, *The* (Columbus, Ind.) *Republic,* Feb. 28, 1976, page number unknown.

3. *The Log* (Columbus [Ind.] High School yearbook), 1916–17, on file at Genealogy Room, Bartholomew County (Ind.) Public Library.

4. Ibid.

5. Thomas A. Hendricks, "Basketballitis Epidemic Now Sweeping Indiana," *The Indianapolis News,* March 13, 1920, pp. 14–15.

6. John Wooden, interview with the author, June 21, 2004, Encino, Calif.

7. Sal Ruibal, "Fieldhouse a Cathedral to High School Hoops," *USA Today,* Feb. 25, 2004, page number unknown.

8. *The Log* (Columbus [Ind.] High School yearbook), 1916–17, on file at Genealogy Room, Bartholomew County (Ind.) Public Library.

9. Found at http://www.crawfordsville.org/citytime.htm

10. Thomas A. Hendricks, "Basketballitis Epidemic Now Sweeping Indiana," *The Indianapolis News,* March 13, 1920, pp. 14–15.

11. Henry S. Wood, "Evolution of Basket Ball in the State Is Traced From Its Early Beginning," *The Indianapolis Star,* March 21, 1926, p. 31.

12. *The Indianapolis Star,* Dec. 1, 1918, page number unknown.

13. "Tech No Match For Local Five: Columbus Shows Rare Form in First Game, Winning 23 to 12: C.H.S. Outclasses Indianapolis Team: Taylor Chief Score Maker for Columbus—Gerhart [*sic*] At Center Scores Points," *The* (Columbus, Ind.) *Herald,* Dec. 14, 1918, page number unknown.

14. "Edinburg Was Easy Picking For Locals: Latter Defeated Former by Score of 65 to 13 Here Last Night," *The* (Columbus, Ind.) *Evening Republican,* Feb. 1, 1919, p. 5.

15. "Franklin Unable to Beat Locals: Winning Record of College Town High School Team Broken By Local Five: Brilliant Playing Marks Most Exciting Contest: Columbus Quintet To Face Another Strong Aggregation Tonight When They Meet Danville Players on Local Floor." *The* (Columbus, Ind.) *Evening Republican,* Feb. 8, 1919, p. 6.

16. "Columbus Downs Hopewell Quint," *The* (Columbus, Ind.) *Evening Republican,* Feb. 15, 1919, p. 5.

17. "Bedford Easy For Columbus: Local Tossers Pile Up Heavy Score on Visitors—Gerhardt Scores Seventeen Baskets," *The* (Columbus, Ind.) *Evening Republican,* March 1, 1919, p. 2.

18. "Gambling Taboo At the Basketball Tournament Here: Any Betting on Games Will Be Followed by Prosecutions, Says Chief Cooper," *The* (Columbus, Ind.) *Evening Republican,* March 7, 1919, p. 1.

19. "Locals 'Doped' For Final Game Of The Tourney: Many People Turned Away from Last Night's Game By Fire Chief Kailor: North Vernon Was Only Practice For Bull Dogs: Hundreds of High School

164

Boys and Girls Parade Streets of City Discussing Basketball Tourney," *The* (Columbus, Ind.) *Evening Republican*, March 8, 1919, pp. 1, 7.

20. "Columbus Wins Third Tourney: Took Seymour Into Camp Easily and Will Take Part in State Tournament," *The* (Columbus, Ind.) *Evening Republican*, sports section, March 10, 1919, p. 2.

21. Ibid.

22. Ibid.

23. "Rochester Five Qualifies: Will Meet Columbus: Fulton County Tossers Eliminate Greencastle by Score of 16 to 8: Bartholomew's Sturdy Lads Show Their Class: Bull Dogs Dispose of South Bend in Easy Manner—Defensive Play of Winners Feature of Contest," *The* (Columbus, Ind.) *Evening Republican*, March 14, 1919, p. 1.

24. "Columbus Bows to Thorntown in Title Play: Bartholomew County Lads Wage Hard Fight, Losing by Score of 20 to 16: Result of Contest in Doubt Until The End," *The* (Columbus, Ind.) *Evening Republican*, March 15, 1919, p. 1.

25. Ibid.

26. "Credit Due Team," Editorials, *The* (Columbus, Ind.) *Evening Republican*, March 17, 1919, p. 4.

27. "Bull Dogs Are Guests of Honor: Banqueted at Tea Room and Highly Praised at Meeting in the City Hall," *The* (Columbus, Ind.) *Evening Republican*, March 19, 1919, p. 2.

28. "Commercials Take Game From Soldiers: Game Was Fast and Interesting and Final Score was 45 to 30; Concordia Defeats Em-Roes," *The* (Columbus, Ind.) *Evening Republican*, sports section, March 20, 1919, p. 2.

2. Non-Skids

1. Bob Nold, "When Wingfoots Flew," *Akron Beacon Journal*, special section, June 30, 1996.

2. John O'Donnell, "Sport Chat," *The* (Bettendorf-Davenport, Iowa) *Times-Democrat*, July 15, 1961, page number unknown.

3. Robert Peterson, *Cages to Jump Shots: Pro Basketball's Early Years* (Lincoln: University of Nebraska Press, 1990), p. 116.

4. "More Honors to Firestone," *The Firestone Non-Skid*, March 9, 1921, page 4.

5. "Firestone's Recreational Leaders Busy," *Akron Beacon Journal,* Jan. 15, 1920, p. 21.

6. Bob Nold, "When Wingfoots Flew," *Akron Beacon Journal,* special section, June 30, 1996.

7. "Firestone Trims Goodrich Quintet: Non-Skids Close Season With Victory Over Circle Basketball Team," *The Firestone Non-Skid,* March 16, 1921, p. 4.

8. "Let's Make This Dance Best," *The Firestone Non-Skid,* March 23, 1921, p. 4.

9. "A.I.A.A. Has 26 Entries," *The Beacon Journal,* March 2, 1921, p. 12.

10. "Annual Banquet Is Night Feature of Business Program: Conferences Held Throughout Afternoon and Evening; Election of Officers to Be Held This Evening," *Erie* (Pa.) *Dispatch,* March 19, 1921, page number unknown.

11. "Girls Ask Split of Gate Receipts," *Akron Beacon Journal,* Jan. 6, 1920, p. 16.

12. "Ready For Second Annual Sport Convention and Tournament of Industrial Association in Akron," *Akron Beacon Journal,* March 11, 1920, p. 22.

13. "A.I.A.A. Tournament Starts Tonight on Y.M.C.A. Court: Three Big Games Arranged For Opening Night's Program—Seventeen Strong Teams Entered in Elimination Process—Nine Games Carded Tomorrow," *The Erie Daily Times,* March 17, 1921, p. 19 (note: several invited teams never showed up).

14. "G.E. Techs First Local Competitor to Be Eliminated: Akron Firestones too Fast and Strong for Light General Electric Apprentices; McFayden and Bond [*sic*] Heavy Scorers," *Erie Dispatch,* March 18, 1921, page number unknown.

15. Title unavailable, *Akron Beacon Journal,* Jan. 21, 1922, p. 8.

3. Salesman

1. Undated clipping from unknown newspaper, but refers to Chuck's season "last year with the Firestone tire team." From Aurilla Cochran Taylor collection.

2. "Concordians Will Meet The Famed Detroit Rayls at College Gym Tonight," *The Fort Wayne News and Sentinel,* Feb. 8, 1919, p. 4.

3. "Man Nobody Knows Is Called 'Great'," *The Detroit News,* Nov. 17, 1940, page number unknown.

4. "Chuck Taylor," Vertical file, Naismith Memorial Basketball Hall of Fame, Springfield, Mass.

5. Pat Harmon, "Basketball's Trick Man," *The Cincinnati Post,* page number and date unknown, but it refers to Chuck's "recent" death, so the year is probably 1969.

6. Marquis Converse, quoted in in-house publication called *Triple Tread News,* as reported in Emily Walzer, "The History of Converse Inc., 1908–1996," an internal house publication prepared by Walzer, a professional archivist, on file at Converse, Inc., North Andover, Mass., p. 5.

7. Craig R. McCoy, "Sneaker," *Lansdale Reporter,* March 1, 1979, page number unknown.

8. *The Bulletin,* September 1969, National Association of Basketball Coaches, as reprinted in *Sporting Goods Bulletin* no. 1, vol. 8, Oct. 3, 1969, an in-house publication of the Converse Rubber Co. Wells coached at Bloomington (Ind.) High School while an undergraduate at nearby Indiana University; he was enshrined in the Naismith Memorial Basketball Hall of Fame as a Contributor himself in 1972.

9. *The Footwear News,* April 13, 1987, page number unknown.

10. Pat Harmon, "Basketball's Trick Man," *The Cincinnati Post,* page number and date unknown, but it refers to Chuck's "recent" death, so the year is probably 1969.

11. Ibid.

12. Murry Nelson, "The Originals: The New York Celtics Invent Modern Basketball" (Bowling Green, Ohio: Bowling Green State University Press, 1999).

13. Naismith Memorial Basketball Hall of Fame, "Hall of Famers" link, www.hoophall.com

14. Cynthia Van Ness, "Victorian Buffalo, speech delivered to the Twentieth Century Club, Buffalo, New York, April 6, 2001," posted on the City of Buffalo web site.

15. "Pro Cage Five To Train Here," *The Richmond* [Ind.] *Item,* Oct. 8, 1926, p. 11.

16. "Taylor Arrives To Put Converse Squad Through Work-outs," *The Richmond Palladium and Sun-Telegram,* Oct. 25, 1926, p. 11.

167

17. "Converse Five Start Practice; Pro Basketball Team To Work On Eagles Gym; Men Report for Drill," *The Richmond Item,* Oct. 27, 1926, p. 5.

18. "Converse Quintet And Richmond Team Scrimmage Tonight," *The Richmond Palladium and Sun-Telegram,* Oct. 29, 1926, p. 13.

19. "Seat Plat Opened For First League Basket Game Nov. 4," *The Richmond Palladium and Sun-Telegram,* Oct. 30, 1926, p. 10.

20. "Pro Basket Team Will Play Here: Converse All-Stars Book Game With Local Team For Tuesday Night—Work Out With Owls: Local Boy in Line-Up," *The Seymour* (Ind.) *Daily Tribune,* Nov. 13, 1926, p. 2.

21. Ibid.

22. "Converse Team Swamps Locals: Professionals Give Interesting Exhibition Against Game Seymour Crew: Show Good Sportsmanship," *Seymour Daily Tribune,* Nov. 17, 1926, p. 2.

23. Ralph H. White, "Jensen Bros. Play Crack Court Crew: Twice State Champs Oppose Converse All Stars at Pennsy Gym Thursday Night," *Terre Haute Tribune,* Dec. 15, 1926, p. 12.

24. William F. Himmelman, Appendix C to Robert Peterson, *Cages to Jump Shots: Pro Basketball's Early Years* (Lincoln: University of Nebraska Press, 1990).

25. Dayton Public Library, Local History Room, e-mail to author, Jan. 10, 2004.

26. "Taylor Coming Long Distance for Game," *The Dayton Journal,* Dec. 17, 1927, p. 7.

27. Preston Hinebaugh, "Dayton Cagers Give World Champions Stiff Battle in Struggle at Coliseum Court: Gem City Quintet Shows Good Form Against Visitors in Second Half," *The Dayton Journal,* sports section, December 18, 1927, p. 1.

28. "2 Dead, 9 Injured in Traffic Crashes," *The Indianapolis Sunday Star,* Oct. 4, 1931, p. 1.

4. The Invisible Pass

1. Aurilla Cochran Taylor collection, publications and dates unknown, but likely from 1950, the year CCNY won the dual championship.

2. Larry Weindruch, e-mail to author, August 7, 2003.

168

3. Pat Harmon, "Basketball's Trick Man," *The Cincinnati Post,* page number and date unknown, but it refers to Chuck's "recent" death, so the year is probably 1969.

4. Reprinted in an ad in the Converse Basketball Yearbooks throughout the 1930s.

5. Radio script, Converse, Inc. archives, North Andover, Mass.

6. Bob Goodell, "Free Hoop 'Clinic' Set At Gym Tonight: Chuck Taylor Will Stage Novel Demonstration of Hoop Fundamentals for Fans," publication and date unknown, from Aurilla Cochran Taylor collection.

7. "Chuck Taylor Proves He Has Lost None Of His Cleverness," *The Atchison* (Kan.) *Daily Globe,* Dec. 6, 1945, p. 8.

8. Converse Basketball Yearbook, 1922 edition, foreword.

9. J. B. (Johnny) McClendon, "Two in the Corner Offense," Converse Basketball Yearbook, 1957 edition, p. 36.

10. Converse Basketball Yearbook, 1937–38 edition; also others.

11. "Chuck Taylor," Vertical file, Naismith Memorial Basketball Hall of Fame, Springfield, Mass.

12. Grady Lewis, telephone interview with the author, August 2003.

13. http://nabc.collegesports.com

14. Advertising Budget, Fiscal Year 1949, Converse Rubber Co., Converse, Inc. archives, North Andover, Mass.

15. Clipping from Aurilla Cochran Taylor collection, publication and date unknown. A clipping from *The Indianapolis Star* edition of August 3, 1938 in the same collection makes brief reference to the same tournament and Chuck's role in it.

16. www.converse.com/history

17. "Sole Man: Most Popular Basketball Shoe Developed by Columbus' Carl Hertel and Chuck Taylor," *The* (Columbus, Ind.) *Republic,* March 8, 1987, page number unknown.

18. "As Converse shuts down U.S. production of Chuck Taylor All Star shoes, Hoosiers remember the original Chuck," by Abe Aamidor, *The Indianapolis Star,* March 14, 2001, page E-1.

5. Special Service

1. Ty Cobb, "Inside Stuff," *Nevada State Journal,* Dec. 2, 1941, p. 8.

2. Minutes, First Meeting on Athletics of the Joint Army and Navy Committee on Welfare and Recreation, June 6, 1941, p. 2. Munitions Building, Washington D.C. National Archives and Records Administration II, College Park, Md., RG 160 Records of Headquarters Special Services Division General Records 1941–45, 353.8 Research File-Sports. (Box number not recorded.)

3. "Special Services Division" handbook, February 15, 1944. National Archives and Records Administration II, College Park, Md., RG 160 Records of Headquarters Special Services Division General Records 1941–45, 353.8 Research File-Sports. (Box number not recorded.)

4. Donald W. Rominger, Jr., "The Impact of the United States Government Sports and Physical Training Policy on Organized Athletics During WWII" (Ph.D. diss., Oklahoma State University, May 1976), p. 252.

5. Minutes, First Meeting on Athletics of the Joint Army and Navy Committee on Welfare and Recreation, June 6, 1941, p. 3. Munitions Building, Washington D.C. National Archives and Records Administration II, College Park, Md., RG 160 Records of Headquarters Special Services Division General Records 1941–45, 353.8 Research File-Sports. (Box number not recorded.)

6. "Office of the Director, Special Services Division file SPSPA 353.8 (6-1-43) subject basketball," National Archives and Records Administration II, College Park, Md., RG 160 Records of Headquarters Special Services Division General Records 1941–45, 353.8 Research File-Sports. (Box number not recorded.)

7. Donald W. Rominger, Jr., "The Impact of the United States Government Sports and Physical Training Policy on Organized Athletics During WWII" (Ph.D. diss., Oklahoma State University, May 1976), p. 1.

8. HickokSports.com, Sports Biographies: Hinkle, "Tony" (Paul D.).

9. Jim L. Sumner, "Hoosier Basketball in North Carolina," *Traces* magazine, Fall 1993, Indiana Historical Society, p. 8.

10. "Athletics and Recreation: A Model 60-Day Program, draft, Prepared by Special Services Division, Army Service Forces, 22 Sept 1944," National Archives and Records Administration II, College Park, Md., RG 160 Records of Headquarters Special Services Divi-

sion General Records 1941–45, 353.8 Research File-Sports. (Box number not recorded.)

11. Paul D. Hinkle, "Basketball Is Best Sport for Morale, Says Paul Hinkle, Great Lakes' Coach," (Reno) *Nevada State Journal,* Jan. 3, 1943, p. 52.

12. Charles C. Spink & Son, signature illegible, to Mr. Frederick Osborne, dated June 13, 1941. National Archives and Records Administration II, College Park, Md., RG 160 Records of Headquarters Special Services Division General Records 1941–45, 353.8 Research File-Sports. (Box number not recorded; see also the American Philosophical Society based in Philadelphia, which has a substantial collection of Osborn's papers, including wartime diary. The Society calls Osborn an important "administrator, humanist and scientist" on its web site.)

13. John L. Dedeick, Sporting Enterprises, to Director, Special Services Division, Army Service Forces, War Department, Washington, D.C., dated Jan. 8, 1944. National Archives and Records Administration II, College Park, Md., RG 160 Records of Headquarters Special Services Division General Records 1941–45, 353.8 Research File-Sports. (Box number not recorded.)

14. National Personnel Records Center, Military Personnel Records, St. Louis, to author, Nov. 6, 2003.

15. "Lt. Taylor to Interview Navy Pilot Candidates," *The* (Columbus, Ind.) *Republic,* Feb. 9, 1944, page number unknown.

16. Donald W. Rominger, Jr., "From Playing Field to Battleground: The United States Navy V-5 Program in World War II," *Journal of Sport History,* vol. 12, no. 3 (Winter 1985), p. 256.

17. Ibid., p. 263.

18. Matt Blessing, Head of Special Collections and University Archives, Marquette University Libraries, e-mail to author, Nov. 25, 2003.

19. "The Evolution of and Ever-evolving Army Sports Program," United States Air Force Museum, Public Affairs Division, Wright-Patterson Air Force Base, Ohio; found at www.armymwr.com/portal/recreation/sportsandfitness/history/history.asp

20. Minutes, First Meeting of the Subcommittee on Athletics of the Joint Army and Navy Committee on Welfare and Recreation, June 6, 1941, Washington, D.C. Found at National Archives and

Records Administration II, College Park, Md., RG 160 Records of Headquarters Special Services Division General Records 1941–45, 353.8 Research File-Sports. (Box number not recorded.)

21. "Constructing a Postwar World: The G.I. Roundtable Series in Context—Background and Context," the American Historical Association, found at www.theaha.org/Projects/GIroundtable/Analysis/Analysis1_Context.htm; Christopher P. Loss, "Between Citizens and State: World War II, Education and the GI Bill," Miller Center of Public Affairs, 20th Century Colloquium, University of Virginia, Dec. 5, 2003, found at http://www.americanpoliticaldevelopment.org/townsquare/print_res/in_progress/loss.pdf

6. Air-Tecs

1. "Taylor Sweats Pounds Off Air-Tec Players," *The Dayton Herald,* Dec. 5, 1944, p. 22.

2. "ATSC Forms Star Quintet: Taylor Plans National Schedule For Soldiers," Dec. 3, 1944, *The* (Dayton, Ohio) *Journal-Herald,* p. 17.

3. Bob Hunter, "Final Four was no big deal back in '39," *The Columbus Dispatch,* March 24, 1999, found at www.dispatch.com/bball/98–99season/march99/hunt0324.html

4. Chuck Taylor, "Keyport, Asbury Park Players to Assist 'Chuck' Taylor in County Basketball Clinic," *Long Branch* (N.J.) *Daily Record,* December 1936, exact date and page number unknown.

5. Sam Butz, newspaper interview, from Aurilla Cochran Taylor collection, publication unknown, circa 1937.

6. Private communication from Jim Ciborski, Wright-Patterson Air Force Base historian, 2003.

7. Donald W. Rominger, Jr., "The Impact of the United States Government Sports and Physical Training Policy on Organized Athletics During WWII" (Ph.D. diss., Oklahoma State University, May 1976), p. 249.

8. Diana Eddleman Lenzi, *Dike Eddleman: Illinois' Greatest Athlete* (Champaign, Ill.: Sports Publishing Inc., a division of Sagamore Publishing Inc., 1997), p. 63. Luisetti often is credited with inventing the one-handed jump shot.

9. "The Air Tecs," *Wright Field Take-Off* (post newspaper), vol. 3, no. 20, p. 10, Dec. 30, 1944.

10. "Employee 5 Books Fast Air Tecs," *Postings* (official publication of the Fairfield Air Technical Service Command), vol. 3, no. 44, Jan. 26, 1945, p. 3.

11. "Air Tecs Put On A Show," *Dayton Daily News,* Feb. 12, 1945, p. 14. The "Coliseum" where the Air-Tecs beat the Aviators almost certainly was the same venue where Taylor met the Original Celtics during the 1927–28 season as a member of the Dayton Kellys.

12. Ibid.

13. "Chuck Taylor Proves He Has Lost None of His Cleverness," The *Atchison* (Kan.) *Daily Globe,* Dec. 16, 1945, p. 8. Wright-Patterson Air Force Base does not have independent verification of this tally, and it's not known how many games the Air-Tecs dropped.

14. "Air-Tecs Take 2 Coast Wins," *Dayton Daily News,* sports section, Feb. 25, 1945, p. 2.

15. "Air-Tecs Get Service 'Invite,'" *Dayton Daily News,* Feb. 9, 1945, p. 25.

16. "Air-Tec Travels End But May Play Here," *Dayton Daily News,* sports section, March 3, 1945, p. 3.

17. William F. Himmelman, Appendix C to Robert Peterson, *Cages to Jump Shots: Pro Basketball's Early Years* (Lincoln: University of Nebraska Press, 1990).

18. "Zollners Swamp Acme, 78–52: Dayton Trails Throughout In Pro Title Tilt," *Dayton Daily News,* sports section, March 25, 1945, p. 1.

19. "Air Tecs Win In Sub Role," *The Dayton Herald,* March 5, 1945, p. 10.

20. "Tecs, Subbing For Buckeyes, Beat Aviators," *Dayton Daily News,* March 5, 1945, p. 14.

21. William F. Himmelman, Appendix C to Robert Peterson, *Cages to Jump Shots: Pro Basketball's Early Years* (Lincoln: University of Nebraska Press, 1990).

22. "Acme Starters Still In Doubt," *Dayton Daily News,* March 9, 1945, p. 25.

23. "3 Regular Players in Acme Lineup Against Chicago Here," *Dayton Daily News,* sports section, March 11, 1945, p. 2.

24. "New Acme Lineup To Be Seen Sunday In National Preview," *Dayton Daily News,* sports section, March 18, 1945, p. 2.

25. Harry Wilson, "World Cage Who's Who: Gates, Carpenter Crowd McDermott," *Chicago Herald-American,* March 15, 1945, p. 6.

26. "Tourney Win Counts More For Aviators," *Dayton Daily News,* March 19, 1945, p. 14.

7. World Tourney

1. John Schleppi, "Chicago's World Tournament of Professional Basketball 1939–48," found at http://www.AAFLA.org/SportsLibrary/NASSH_Proceedings/NP1989/NP1989Zd.pdf

2. Keith Brehm, "Hartford, Dayton Fill World Cage Field," *Chicago Herald-American,* March 5, 1945, p. 6.

3. "Pro Cage in Playoffs: Gears Open at Sheboygan," *Chicago Herald-American,* March 6, 1945, p. 6.

4. "Sheboygan To Appear Here For First Time," *The Dayton Herald,* Dec. 8, 1944, p. 26.

5. "Quarterfinals Program Tops in World Cage," *Chicago Herald-American,* March 8, 1945, p. 6.

6. Keith Brehm, "Champions Put on Spot in World Cage Meet," *Chicago Herald-American,* March 10, 1945, p. 6.

7. Harry Wilson, "World Cage Who's Who," *Chicago Herald-American,* March 15, 1945, p. 6.

8. Keith Brehm, "(Pistons), Gears, Rens, Acmes Advance: Await World Cage Semifinals Today," *Chicago Herald-American,* March 23, 1945, p. 6.

9. "Acme (Air-Tecs) Jump To Pro Semifinals," *The Dayton Herald,* March 22, 1945, p. 22. There were several other headlines that referred to the team's dual identity.

10. Joe Goldstein, "Rumblings: The Brooklyn Five," Nov. 19, 2003, found at http://espn.go.com/classic/s/basketball_scandals_rumblings.html

11. Alan Rubenstein, "College Basketball—Looking at NCAA Hoops Scandals," Sept. 18, 2003, found at www.sports-central.org/sports/college_basketball/articles/article196.shtml

12. "Acme, Setting Meet Record With 80–51 Win, Faces Zollners in Finals," *Dayton Daily News,* March 24, 1945, p. 8.

13. "Zollners Swamp Acmes, 78–52: Dayton Trails Throughout In Pro Title Tilt," *Dayton Daily News,* sports section, March 25, 1945, p. 1.

14. Keith Brehm, "Fort Wayne Hailed Tops: Many Marks Set in Cage Tourney," *Chicago Herald-American,* March 27, 1945, p. 6.

15. Jerry Cohen, "Acme (Air-Tecs) Home From World Tourney," *The Dayton Herald,* March 26, 1945, p. 14.

8. "Me"

1. *Total Basketball: The Ultimate Basketball Encylopedia* (Toronto, Ont.: SportClassic Books, 2003), p. 92.

2. http://www.hoophall.com/halloffamers/Rupp.htm

3. John Wooden, interview with the author, Encino, Calif., June 21, 2004.

4. File number 13104, Complaint for Divorce, In the Superior Court of the State of California In and For the County of Los Angeles, filed May 18, 1955.

5. James M. Keys, Public Affairs Officer, Foreign Service Despatch, to the Department of State and United States Information Agency, Ref. CA-6387, February 8, 1957, and dated July 9, 1957; found at National Archives and Records Administration II, RG 59, Central Decimal Files (1955–59), Box 2120.

6. "Buena Charla Ofreció el Técnico Yanqui, Taylor," *Acción* (Montevideo, Uruguay), May 28, 1957, page number unknown.

7. http://www.naia.org/index.html

8. Ed Miller, "Basketball's Forgotten Pioneer," *The Virginian-Pilot,* Feb. 22, 1995, page C1.

9. William E. Parrish, author of "Westminster College: An Informal History, 1851–1999," e-mail to Pat Kirby, Aug. 18, 2003, and forwarded to the author by Mike Odneal, Westminster College spokesman. A picture alluded to in the e-mail shows Chuck, dressed in sweat pants and knit shirt, "passing a ball effortlessly to Rich Autry [15], Westminster player, despite the efforts of Dave Wright to block the pass." It was the invisible pass! Autry graduated from the college in 1960, according to Odneal.

10. William Woods College program, Jan. 9, 1941, and an undated Fulton, Mo. newspaper clipping, both from the Lucy Taylor Hennessey estate.

11. Alan Kimbrell to Lucille Kimbrell, handwritten on The Gunter Hotel stationery in San Antonio, Texas. The letter is undated, but other letters from Alan in the collection were written in 1960 and 1961, based on envelope postmarks where available.

175

12. R. D. "Randy" Cutlip to Lucille Prater Kimbrell, June 6, 1962, from Lucy Taylor Hennessey estate.

13. Marriage Certificate No. 574387, State of Nevada, County of Washoe, recorded Dec. 20, 1962.

14. Roger Mooney, "Giant Step Forward," *Port Charlotte* (Fla.) *Sun,* sports section, July 17, 1996, p. 1.

9. Glory

1. J. D. Clements to Chuck Taylor, March 29, 1969, from the Lucille Taylor Hennessey estate.

2. Charles "Stretch" Murphy to Mr. Lee Williams, Naismith Memorial Basketball Hall of Fame, June 24, 1968, from the Lucy Taylor Hennessey estate.

3. See especially the Introduction to Sandy Padwe, *Basketball's Hall of Fame* (Englewood Cliffs, N.J.: Prentice-Hall, 1970), for the story of how the Hall of Fame was built.

4. Clifford Wells, eulogy for Chuck Taylor, reprinted in *Sporting Goods Bulletin* (in-house Converse publication), No. 1, Volume 8, October 3, 1969.

5. Jackie MacMullan, "The Shoe Fits: The classically simple Chuck Taylor sneaker is still the standard by which all other high-tops are measured," *Ultrasport Review,* April 1987, pp. 77–81.

6. Emily Walzer, "The History of Converse Inc., 1908–1996," an internal house publication prepared by Walzer, a professional archivist, on file at Converse, Inc., North Andover, Mass., p. 21.

7. Frank McGuire, basketball coach at the University of South Carolina, to Mrs. C. H. Taylor, dated April 2, 1970, from the Lucy Taylor Hennessey estate.

8. John O'Donnell, column, *The* (Davenport-Bettendorf, Iowa) *Times-Democrat,* March 19, 1968, pp. 13–14.

9. Lucy Taylor to Lee Williams, executive director of the Naismith Memorial Basketball Hall of Fame, August 8, 1969, from the Lucy Taylor Hennessey estate. This letter appears to be the original letter. It is unknown why the letter was in Lucy's possession at the time of her death.

Appendix

1. Emily Walzer, "The History of Converse Inc., 1908–1996,"

176

an internal house publication prepared by Walzer, a professional archivist, on file at Converse, Inc., North Andover, Mass., p. 6.

2. Robert Peterson, *Cages to Jump Shots: Pro Basketball's Early Years* (Lincoln: University of Nebraska Press, 1990) pp. 41–42.

3. Cameron Kippen, "The History of Sport Shoes," p. 5. Available online at www.curtin.edu.au/curtin/dept/physio/podiatry/sport.html

4. Mary Bellis, "Inventors: Footware and Shoes," found at http://inventors.about.com/library/inventors/blshoe.htm

5. Richard Lapchick, e-mail to author, June 29, 2004.

6. Emily Walzer, "The History of Converse Inc., 1908–1996," an internal house publication prepared by Walzer, a professional archivist, on file at Converse, Inc., North Andover, Mass., p. 15.

7. "Founder and Former Head of Converse Rubber Co. Dies of Heart Trouble at Wheel of Car on Milk St., Boston. Was Remarkable Salesman," *Malden* (Mass.) *Evening News*, Feb. 10, 1931, p. 1.

8. Ibid., p. 5.

9. Stephen Stone obituary, *The Boston Globe*, May 31, 2002, p. D-17.

10. Ellen Pulda, "Converse has high hopes in Jack Purcell shoe," *Footwear News*, Oct. 19, 1987, p. 2. See also "Sports Hall of Fame Adds Four More," *Guelph* (Ontario, Canada) *Mercury*, April 2, 2002, p. B3.

11. Business News, Associated Press, July 4, 1989. Available online at www.nexis.com

12. *Malden Evening News*, undated article, from Converse, Inc. archives, North Andover, Mass.

13. "Leather All Star Progress Report," *Sporting Goods Bulletin* (mimeographed in-house Converse publication), Oct. 3, 1969, p. 2.

14. Emily Walzer, "The History of Converse Inc., 1908–1996," an internal house publication prepared by Walzer, a professional archivist, on file at Converse, Inc., North Andover, Mass., p. 28.

15. "Business and Company Resource Center," Document Number I2501304014, The Gale Group, Inc., Copyright 2003.

16. Bruce Horovitz, "Whose Shoes Will 'Magic' Johnson Don?" *Chicago Sun-Times*, Oct. 5, 1992, p. 45.

17. Gregg Krupa, "Converse Unties Knot with Rodman: Full-time icon, sometimes player, loses $15 million Contract," *The Boston Globe*, March 23, 1999, p. C-1.

18. Emily Walzer, "The History of Converse Inc., 1908–1996,"

an internal house publication prepared by Walzer, a professional archivist, on file at Converse, Inc., North Andover, Mass., p. 34.

19. Ibid., p. 35.

20. Catherine Pritchard, "Converse in step for survival," *Fayetteville* (N.C.) *Observer-Times,* Aug. 25, 1996, p. D-1.

21. "Hoover's Company Profile Database—American Public Companies, 2001, Converse, Inc.," available at www.hoovers.com (subscription required). See also http://galenet.galegroup.com

22. Justin Pope, "Converse seeks the top again; Troubled shoe company tries to recover," *South Bend* (Ind.) *Tribune* (Associated Press wire story), July 12, 2001, p. B10.

23. J. Kyle Foster, "Lumberton's Converse plant closes its doors," *Fayetteville* (N.C.) *Observer-Times,* March 24, 2001, page number not recorded.

24. Hal Bock, "Critics cry foul over name," *Hamilton* (Ontario) *Spectator* (Associated Press wire story), Sept. 26, 2003, p. E-1.

25. Iain Aitch, "Black Spot," *The Independent* (London, England), Dec. 15, 2003, pp. 4–5.

26. Lyrics quoted in "Theme of authenticity found in latest ad by Converse," from Converse TV ad as sung by Mos Def and reported by Rob Walker on National Public Radio, Sept. 25, 2003. Transcript published on www.npr.org

Index

Italicized page numbers refer to illustrations.

180

Index

184

Index

ABRAHAM AAMIDOR

a staff writer for *The Indianapolis Star,* has reported for
The Champaign-Urbana News-Gazette and *The St. Louis
Globe-Democrat.* He is author of *Real Feature Writing* (1999)
and editor of *Real Sports Reporting* (Indiana University Press,
2003). He lives in Carmel, Indiana with his wife, Shirley.